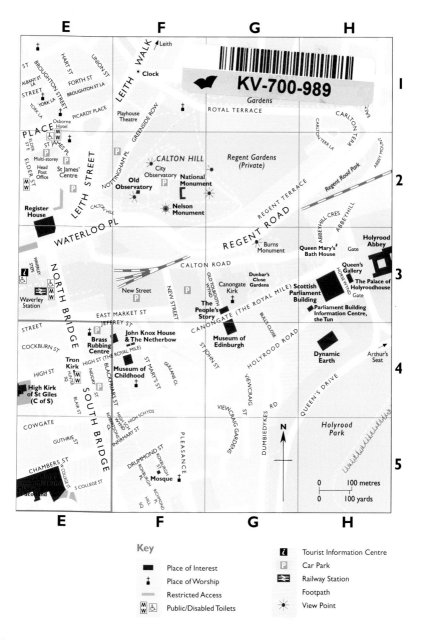

EDINBURGH

...MORE THAN A GUIDE

JARROLD
publishing

EDINBURGH

MORE THAN A GUIDE

ANNIE BULLEN

Acknowledgements
Photography © Jarrold
Publishing by Neil
Jinkerson.
Additional photography
by kind permission of:
Annie Bullen, Edinburgh
Zoo, Hopetoun House,
Kelpie Design, The Royal
Collection © 2005 Her
Majesty Queen Elizabeth
II and The Witchery by
the Castle.

The quote on page 17
from *The Prime of Miss
Jean Brodie* by Muriel
Spark is used by permis-
sion of Penguin Books
and David Higham
Associates.

The publishers wish to
thank Stephen Crowe of
Edinburgh & Lothians
Tourist Board for his
invaluable assistance; also
the many owners of
Edinburgh businesses for
their kindness in allowing
us to photograph their
premises.

All information correct at
time of going to press but
may be subject to change.

Printed in Singapore.
ISBN 0 7117 3593 X 1/05

Designer:
Simon Borrough
Editor:
Angela Royston
**Artwork and walk
maps:**
Clive Goodyer
City maps:
The Map Studio Ltd,
Romsey, Hants.
Main map based on
cartography © George
Philip Ltd.

The routes map on page
100 includes mapping
data licensed from

Mapping
sourced from

**Front cover:
Detail of statue
outside St Giles**

**Title page:
Detail of slate cone
by Andy Goldsworthy,
Royal Botanic Garden**

CONTENTS

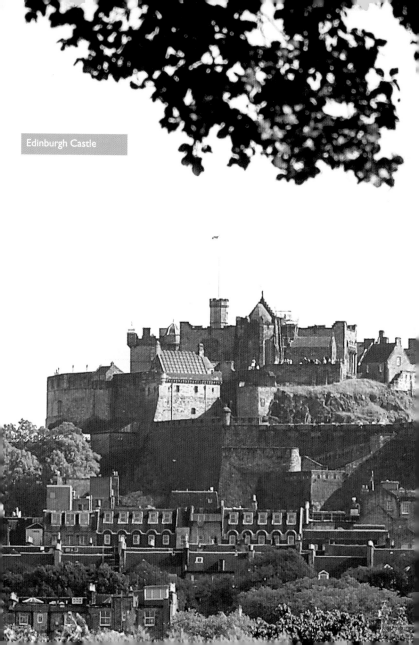

Edinburgh Castle

WELCOME TO EDINBURGH

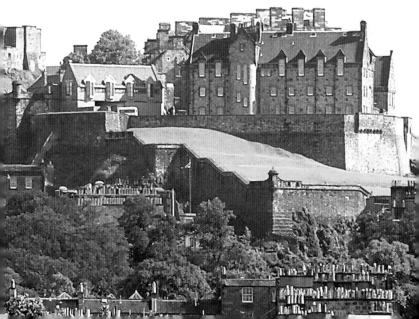

Edinburgh – this beautiful city of the North – has been shaped by a turbulent history that contrasts with its civilized 21st-century image as a place of culture, comfort and excitement. With its massive castle, dramatic on an outcrop of dark rock, and its imposing royal residence, the Palace of Holyroodhouse, Edinburgh's heritage underlies the café culture, the excellent museums and galleries, the shops, restaurants and the neo-classical architecture.

The so-called New Town to the north is elegant and symmetrical. It was built well over 200 years ago of solid grey granite, wrought iron and soft red sandstone to accommodate an ever-increasing population. The Old Town, with its overhanging tall tenement buildings, winding streets and closes, is picturesque and full of interest. Here the skirl of bagpipes and swirl of the piper's kilt is not only a performance put on for the benefit of tourists, but also an affirmation of centuries of history and tradition.

Anta (page 68)

Edinburgh, Old Town and New, enchants visitors – they fall in love with this wonderful city whose lively shopping and cafés sit easily in its ancient streets, where bloody battles, royal pageant and local custom have all been played out. For centuries artists and writers have lived here, gaining inspiration from Edinburgh's dramatic past. That artistic tradition lives on in the annual international festival, famous the world over, when for one month the city gives itself up to culture of all kinds from film and performances by top orchestras to theatre and off-beat art.

This is a city whose history stretches back from before the early kings of Scotland and forward into the 21st century to encompass some of the best modern museums and art galleries in the world. Princes Street and the Royal Mile are names known throughout the world, but it is only when you walk down these famous thoroughfares that you begin to absorb Edinburgh's special atmosphere and understand why so many visitors are drawn back here time and time again.

Flower stall

HIGHLIGHTS

Edinburgh Castle

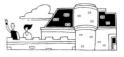

Magnificent upon its high rocky outcrop, Edinburgh Castle dominates the streets below at every turn. It's the obvious starting point for visitors in a city that is full of interest. Walk uphill towards it, turning back, once you reach the esplanade, to look at the buildings and the distant Pentland Hills spread out below and beyond. This is the highlight for many visitors – but there are plenty more.

CASTLE IN THE AIR
Castlehill; map B4–C5

With sheer rock on three sides you must climb up towards the Castle from the east, along the Royal Mile or up steep Ramsay Lane from The Mound (map C4). Pause to get your breath – the road winds uphill all the way once inside the gatehouse to various parts of the citadel.

A guided tour is included in the entrance fee or you can wander round the various buildings, museums, batteries, chapel, the palace and National War Memorial as you please. For a small fee the extremely good audioguides will tell as little or as much as you want to know about any particular part of the Castle. Be ready to jump out of your skin at one o'clock as a cannon is fired from the battlements each day except Sunday, startling birds and tourists alike. You'll see crowds gathering by the gun just before firing time.

The Castle has been fortress and home to Scotland's kings and queens. In the palace you'll see the cupboard-sized room where James VI (James I of England and Scotland) was born and, if you don't mind the claustrophobic shuffle up winding stairs, the magnificent crown jewels – the sceptre, the sword and the crown, together known as the Honours of Scotland. Beautiful in its simplicity is St Margaret's Chapel, the oldest building in the complex, constructed in the early 12th century. Outside stands giant Mons Meg, the famous 600-year-old siege gun said to have fired an enormous shot 3 kilometres (2 miles). On a clear day the views from this part of the Castle are stupendous.

Open: daily; Apr–Oct: 9.30–18.00; Nov–Mar: 9.30–17.00
Entry: around £10 (covers all the attractions within the Castle); audioguides extra
Further information: pages 36–37

WHEN THE EARTH MOVED

Landscape architect Charles Jencks' radical *Landform Ueda* at the Scottish National Gallery of Modern Art scooped the UK's largest arts award, the Gulbenkian Prize. The 21-metre (70-foot) stepped mound linking three crescent-shaped pools is so popular that some areas of turf have had to be replaced. Visitors come from far and wide to walk round the Landform, built to represent natural forces.

The Palace of Holyroodhouse

VISIT THE ROYALS

The Palace of Holyroodhouse; map H3

When that cold and clammy haar (you'll know what it is if it blows in during your visit) wraps itself round the Castle, life isn't comfortable for anyone. So it isn't really surprising that the Royals decamped to the much cosier guest house of Holyrood Abbey, founded by King David I in 1128. Soon an extra wing was added until, by the time of the Stuarts, a brand new palace had been built here. Now the Palace of Holyroodhouse is the official residence in Scotland of the Royal Family.

The oldest part of the building is what interests most visitors, who want to see the bedchamber where Mary Queen of Scots slept and the adjoining room where her secretary Rizzio was fatally stabbed as they sat together. There's an interesting collection of Mary's needlework and other pieces including jewellery and paintings relating to that period. You'll see the Great Gallery with its picture-hung walls and the elegant Morning Drawing Room during your tour of the rest of the building. Guided tours are compulsory between November and the end of March, otherwise you can walk around at your own pace.

Sharing the site is the wonderful, recently opened Queen's Gallery – designed and built by Scottish architects and craftsmen and a beautiful space in which to show off paintings and other works of art from the Royal Collection.

Open: Palace and Queen's Gallery: daily; Apr–end Oct: 9.30–18.00; Nov–end Mar: 9.30–16.30; Palace or Gallery may close during these times – check before you visit

Entry: Palace, under £10 (including audioguide); Queen's Gallery, under £5; combined ticket, over £10

Further information: pages 46–47

Dragon in Lawnmarket

DO THE ART

No matter that your tastes range from the Italian Renaissance to the French Impressionists, from portraits to post-modern sculpture, you'll find some of the finest art galleries in the world right in the city centre – the National Gallery of Scotland (linked to the Royal Scottish Academy Building) (map C3 and C4) and the National Portrait Gallery (map D2). The National Gallery of Modern Art and the Dean Gallery (the latter home to the work of Eduardo Paolozzi) are in Belford Road, 15 minutes walk from the centre. A shuttle bus runs regularly between all the galleries.

Open: daily; 10.00–17.00, late night Thu 10.00–19.00
Entry: free
Further information: pages 35, 45, 53

GO THE EXTRA MILE

You'll hear a lot about the tenement buildings of the Old Town; walk the length of the Royal Mile (map D4 to G3) from the Castle to Holyrood, taking time to look up at the tall buildings and explore some of the narrow closes and wynds that open out onto the main street. Castlehill, Lawnmarket and the High Street are the busiest sections of the Royal Mile. Canongate, towards the lower end, seems quieter. Here is where you'll find The People's Story, an excellent small museum telling you much about the lives of ordinary people of Edinburgh and the Old Town area.

Henry Moore sculpture, National Gallery of Modern Art

Jenners

SHOP IN STYLE

Very dear to the hearts of most Edinburgh women – and many men too – is Jenners, the world's oldest department store and still remarkable today. It's a landmark in Princes Street (map D3), with a wonderful decorated façade standing out from the other modern shop fronts. Inside, all is wood, marble and galleried landings. Once inside you might find it hard to navigate, but a voyage of discovery like this is worth the exploration.

Open: daily; Mon, Wed, Fri, Sat 9.00–18.00, Tue 9.30–18.00, Thu 9.00–20.00, Sun 11.00–17.00
Further information: pages 41, 62

GO GREEN

The Royal Botanic Garden in Inverleith Road, a short walk (15 to 20 minutes) from the city centre, offers hours of pleasure. There are acres to stroll in, a collection of glasshouses to rival those at Kew, a Chinese pavilion, heath garden, herbaceous borders and much more, including a wonderful alpine collection.

You are sure to admire the striking entrance gates designed by Ben Tindall and sculptures by Andy Goldsworthy and Ian Hamilton Finlay. You can take a picnic to eat in the gardens or have a relaxing lunch at The Terrace Café.

Open: daily; 10.00 – between 16.00 and 19.00 depending on season
Entry: free (charge to visit glasshouses)
Further information: page 48

Slate cone, Royal Botanic Garden

DID THE EARTH MOVE?

It probably will if you visit the acclaimed Dynamic Earth in Holyrood Road (map H4). Here you get a chance to experience volcanoes, earthquakes, icebergs and the rainforest. This Millennium project which has become one of Edinburgh's top tourist attractions is full of interactive excitement and interest.

Open: Apr–Oct: daily, 10.00–17.00 (18.00 during Jul and Aug); Nov–Mar: Wed–Sun 10.00–17.00
Entry: under £10
Further information: pages 35–36

BE BEWITCHED

'Eye of newt and toe of frog' is what you definitely won't get if you choose to eat at The Witchery by the Castle in Castlehill (map D4), although the restaurant is certainly atmospheric. The food is delicious but pricey, although the lunchtime and pre-theatre set menu offers very good value. Café Hub, nearby in Lawnmarket (map D4), is another good lunchtime (and evening) venue. If you're over in the New Town try Glass and Thompson in Dundas Street (map C1) for a lunchtime snack or Henderson's (innovative vegetarian) in Hanover Street (map C2). The best scones are said to be at the Queen Street Café in the National Portrait Gallery (map D2).

Further information: pages 70–79

Wrought ironwork in the New Town

ENJOY THE ARCHITECTURE

You've seen the Old Town with its narrow streets and tall tenements; for a real flavour of the architecture of the New Town, stroll down to St Stephen Street having a good look at the elegant and expensive houses of the Royal Circus and Heriot Row (map B1 and C2) on the way. There are good cafés and pubs in this area. Nearby Dundas Street (map C1) is the place to explore if you enjoy buying, or just browsing through, paintings and antiques.

ABSORB THE HISTORY

If you think museums dull, you'll change your mind after a visit to the Museum of Scotland in Chambers Street (map E5). This sandstone building, which dominates the corner of the street, houses some of the most exciting exhibits ever to tell a nation's history. You can also walk through to the linked Royal Museum and look at the wacky Millennium Clock.

Open: daily; Mon–Sat 10.00–17.00 (20.00 on Tue), Sun 12.00–17.00
Entry: free
Further information: pages 43–44, 50

Stockbridge Old Market

Greyfriars Bobby

WIPE AWAY A TEAR

You've almost certainly heard of Greyfriars Bobby, the faithful little dog who sat vigil by his master's grave for several years. His statue stands just outside Greyfriars Kirk in Candlemaker Row (map D5); the churchyard where he and his master lie is just behind.
Further information: page 39

CITY OF WRITERS

Edinburgh, where Robbie Burns and Walter Scott lived and wrote, where Percy Bysshe Shelley was married and William Hazlitt divorced, home to J.K. Rowling and Alexander McCall Smith, creator of the *No. 1 Ladies Detective Agency,* has become the world's first official City of Literature. The city's claim was confirmed by UNESCO in October 2004, and there's no doubt that the honour is well bestowed.

You step off the train at Waverley Station, named after the series of novels written by Sir Walter Scott, seen by many as the father of the historical novel. You can't miss his 61-metre (200-foot) high monument, the largest ever built for a writer, in Princes Street. The acid wit of Muriel Spark is nowhere more evident than in her famous Edinburgh novel, *The Prime of Miss Jean Brodie:* 'One's prime is elusive. You little girls … must be on the alert to recognize your prime … you must then live it to the full.'

Scott Monument

Sundial created by Ian
Hamilton Finlay

A darker Edinburgh is portrayed in
Irvine Welsh's *Trainspotting*, while
Inspector Rebus solves crimes commit-
ted here in Ian Rankin's series of popular
novels. Deacon Brodie, the outwardly
respectable but secretly criminal
Edinburgh character, was the inspiration
for Robert Louis Stevenson's novel
Dr Jekyll and Mr Hyde.

Edinburgh was the home for a while
to poets Wilfred Owen and Siegfried
Sassoon, sent here to recover from shell
shock during the First World War. Their
story was the inspiration for Pat Barker's
award-winning 1991 novel *Regeneration*.

More recently, Edinburgh's Canongate
Books published Yann Martel's award
winner *Life of Pi*, which won the 2002
Man Booker Prize.

Robert Burns collected and wrote
around 200 songs and ballads in the

SET IN STONE

Poet and artist Ian Hamilton
Finlay developed so-called
concrete poetry, where the
words on the page rely as
much on their visual impact as
their ideas, when he lived and
worked in Edinburgh in the
1960s. Now his garden Little
Sparta (see page 90) outside
the city is a place of pilgrim-
age for many, although some
of his work can be seen at the
Scottish Gallery of Modern
Art in Belford Road and in the
Royal Botanic Garden.

Scottish dialect in the late 18th century and conducted a passionate affair – by words on paper – with 'Clarinda' (Agnes MacLehose), who is buried in the city in Canongate Kirk (map G3).

Thomas Carlyle, social prophet, historian and critic, was an Edinburgh man, and James Boswell studied at the university.

In the 20th century, poets Hugh MacDiarmid (born Christopher Murray Grieve) and Sydney Goodsir Smith were nurtured in the city, while Sorley Maclean (who died in 1996) taught here and did much to restore the tradition of writing in the Gaelic.

'Concrete' poet Ian Hamilton Finlay, writer, gardener and sculptor, who lives and gardens just outside the city, had much influence over Edinburgh's literary life in the late 20th century. The work of another great gardener and writer, Charles Jencks, can be seen in the shape of *Landform Ueda* outside the National Gallery of Modern Art (see page 9).

DARK INSPIRATION

Deacon William Brodie was a pillar of the community by day – and a villainous burglar by night. Eventually his crimes caught up with him and he was hanged on a gibbet of his own design in the Grassmarket. His near-schizophrenic character was the inspiration for Robert Louis Stevenson's *Dr Jekyll and Mr Hyde*. There's a pub named after him in Lawnmarket on the Royal Mile.

PLANNING YOUR VISIT

The contrast between the sombre granite elegance of the New Town and the remaining towering tenements, winding closes and narrow charm of the Old Town should bring a feeling of disunity to the city. Instead there's a unique sense of time, the new growing out of the old, with interesting developments at every step.

The more you explore, the more you discover. Here are a few suggestions to help you find your way around this most exciting of cities, where history, art and café-culture blend together in an exciting mix.

Edinburgh Castle and Princes Street Gardens

DAY ONE

Start with a stroll down Princes Street (map B4–E3), once an exclusive residential development and now a busy shopping area. The shops are on one side only – the green lawns and colourful flowerbeds of Princes Street Gardens give a feeling of space unusual

National Gallery of Scotland

in a city. Make your way towards The Mound (map C3–4). Before you start the gentle climb up to the Castle you could look in the National Gallery (map C4) where some of the world's great paintings are hung. Entry is free, so call in as often as time and inclination allow.

Walk uphill, following the winding road to Edinburgh Castle. The entry kiosk is on the esplanade. Guided tours are included in the entry price; if you prefer to go free range it's a good idea to rent

an audioguide, which allows you to move at your own pace. The café in the Castle is excellent as are the loos, which almost merit a visit of their own. There's much to see in the Castle and it will probably be time for lunch (see pages 70–79) when you emerge.

As you stroll down the Royal Mile, before or after lunch, divert to Victoria Street (map D5), leading down to the open, partly cobbled area known as the Grassmarket. Here you'll find many

Victoria Street

Grassmarket

'body-snatchers' Burke and Hare had their den in this area in the early 19th century. Their victims would be lured to their death and their bodies sold to physician Robert Knox for his research.

Mary Queen of Scots

There's some bloody history too at the Palace of Holyroodhouse (see pages 46–47) at the end of the Royal Mile. This is where much of the drama of Mary Queen of Scots was played out, and a tour of her apartments in this dramatic building, still a royal residence, shouldn't be missed. If you have the energy (refresh yourself at the excellent café here), visit the adjoining Queen's Gallery, housing changing displays from the Royal Collection and a work of art in its own right.

colourful shops, restaurants and cafés. The Grassmarket looks peaceful enough these days but Edinburgh's gallows were built here and it was once the site of public executions. The notorious

DAYS TWO AND THREE

Even if you managed to squeeze all the suggestions above into one day, Edinburgh has plenty more up her sleeve; here are some 'pick-and-mix' suggestions for the rest of your visit.

Hit the heights

Climb the steps from Waterloo Place (map F3) up to the extraordinary monument-covered Calton Hill (see pages 33–34). Here you get a panoramic view of the city and its surroundings, from Arthur's Seat to the Castle and across the New Town. Alternatively you could visit the Camera Obscura (see pages 34–35) at Castlehill, where you'll be rewarded with more great views. You need to be fairly fit to climb to the top of the Scott Monument (see page 52) in Princes Street – but what a sense of achievement when you do.

Visit Leith

Leith, Edinburgh's port, is a transformed place these days. Smart new shops, restaurants and the Ocean Terminal complex, with *Britannia* (see page 52)

moored alongside, are a world away from the crumbling docklands of old. You might like to stroll the few kilometres (a mile or two) from Princes Street along Leith Walk (map F1), or hop on a bus (clearly marked Ocean Terminal) to enjoy a few hours by the sea.

Pictures of people

The red sandstone exterior of the National Portrait Gallery in Queen Street was modelled on the Doge's Palace in Venice. Inside the main hall, every surface is painted with scenes from Scottish history and pictures of famous Scots. There are changing and permanent exhibitions and portraits which cover centuries of history. It's just a 15-minute walk westwards from here to the Dean Gallery and National Gallery of Modern Art (see page 35). If that sounds too far, a shuttle bus will drop you there.

A short history of time

Some sense of the immense scale of time before mankind appeared, and the huge changes that have happened since

Dean Gallery

we have lived on the Earth, can be gleaned from the superb displays at the Museum of Scotland in Chambers Street (map E5) in the Old Town. If ever a museum brought history to life, this one does.

Harvey Nichols, St Andrew Square

Shop in style

It's almost obligatory to visit Jenners (see page 41) in Princes Street. If fashion is what you like, make a beeline for George Street, full of designer clothes shops, with more top designer names along the north side of St Andrew Square. See the shopping guide on pages 58–69 for more ideas.

Walk to the gardens

A walk out to the Royal Botanic Garden (see page 48) is something to enjoy on a fine day. Make your way back to the city centre by way of the old 'village' of Stockbridge, which still retains its individual atmosphere and is home to many of the more colourful shops in the city. There's a Bohemian feel to the area – especially along the Glenogle Road where the 'Stockbridge Colonies', rows of houses built for craftsmen, still have trade symbols marked on their gable ends.

Hop on a bus

City sightseeing tours with interesting and amusing commentary leave Waverley Bridge (map D3) throughout the day. This is a great way to familiarize yourself with the geography of Edinburgh and to get a feel for some of the events that have shaped the city. Simply buy your ticket at the kiosk by the bridge and hop on your chosen bus. The tickets are valid for 24 hours, so you can climb off to visit sights along the way – a good idea if you don't relish walking up Castlehill.

Royal Botanic Garden

WALKS

There are plenty of excellent guided walks in Edinburgh (see pages 82–83), but if you want to go it alone you could try these three strolls. They show you some of the grandest architecture and at the same time take you to out-of-the-way but interesting parts of the city.

ROYAL BOTANIC GARDEN WALK

The Royal Botanic Garden is one of the best in the world – and within pleasant walking distance of the city centre. This walk takes you through some of Edinburgh's finest streets and through the 'village' of Stockbridge before a short stroll along the Water of Leith to the Botanic Garden.

Start in Charlotte Square (map A3) with its grand Georgian buildings, leaving by Charlotte Street on the east side of the square. Cross over into Forres Street, which will take you to Moray Place, another architectural tour de force. Leave Moray Place along Doune Terrace and turn left into Gloucester Street before crossing over to St Stephen Street.

You are now in Stockbridge, a sunny suburb with a villagey feel. Walk along until you see Clarence Street on your left. Follow this road to the end, crossing over into Saxe-Coburg Place with its central gardens. At the very top you'll find a path taking you down steps into Glenogle Road with its parallel rows of

Moray Place

Glenogle Road

'Stockbridge Colonies', houses built in 1861 for local artisans. Some have trade symbols on their gable ends. Walk along Glenogle Road, turn left into Bell Place and cross the Water of Leith over a wooden bridge. Turn left onto the footpath – the Water of Leith Walkway. At the road turn right and cross over into Arboretum Place, where you'll see signs to the west entrance of the Botanic Garden (see page 48).

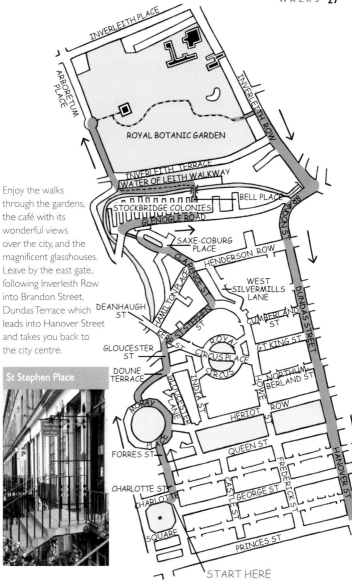

Enjoy the walks through the gardens, the café with its wonderful views over the city, and the magnificent glasshouses. Leave by the east gate, following Inverleith Row into Brandon Street, Dundas Terrace which leads into Hanover Street and takes you back to the city centre.

INVERLEITH PLACE

ARBORETUM PLACE

INVERLEITH ROW

ROYAL BOTANIC GARDEN

INVERLEITH TERRACE
WATER OF LEITH WALKWAY

BELL PLACE

BRANDON ST

STOCKBRIDGE COLONIES
GLENOGLE ROAD

SAXE-COBURG PLACE

CLARENCE ST

HENDERSON ROW

WEST SILVERMILLS LANE

DUNDAS STREET

DEANHAUGH ST

HAMILTON PLACE

KERR ST

ST STEPHEN ST

CUMBERLAND ST

GT KING ST

ROYAL CIRCUS

CIRCUS PLACE

NORTHUMBERLAND ST

GLOUCESTER ST

DOUNE TERRACE

GLOUCESTER LANE

INDIA ST

HOWE ST

St Stephen Place

MORAY PLACE

HERIOT ROW

FORRES ST

QUEEN ST

FREDERICK ST

HANOVER ST

CHARLOTTE ST

CASTLE ST

GEORGE ST

CHARLOTTE SQUARE

PRINCES ST

START HERE

DEAN VILLAGE WALK

Edinburgh has some of the best art galleries in the world. The Dean Gallery and the Scottish National Gallery of Modern Art are across the road from each other a little way out of the city near Dean Village, once a mill area and still picturesque, set in a

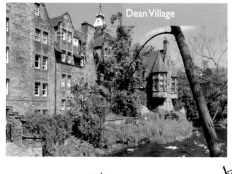
Dean Village

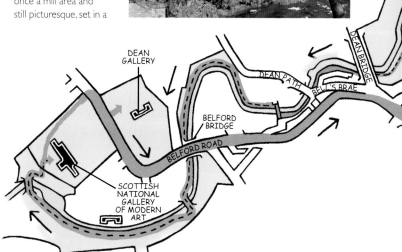

DEAN GALLERY

DEAN PATH

BELL'S BRAE

DEAN BRIDGE

BELFORD BRIDGE

BELFORD ROAD

SCOTTISH NATIONAL GALLERY OF MODERN ART

deep gorge with narrow cobbled streets and tall buildings. You can reach the galleries along the Water of Leith Walkway, exploring Dean Village on the way.

Start in Queen Street from the National Portrait Gallery, which you might like to visit first (see page 53). Cross Queen Street and turn left, walking until you reach Queen Street Gardens West.

Turn right down here into Howe Street, following the road left through the centre of the imposing Royal Circus. Take N.W. Circus Place and follow it into Kerr Street until you see Saunders Street on your left. Turn down here. At the end you'll see a footpath onto the Water of Leith Walkway. Follow this westwards (upriver),

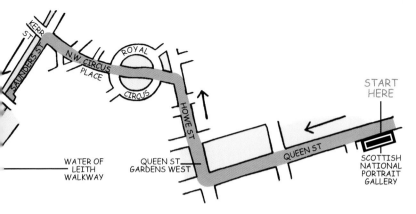

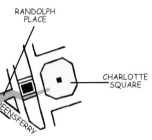

Scottish National Gallery of Modern Art

exploring the village of Dean on the way. Once you've walked under Belford Bridge follow the path along the curve of the river (you'll cross it once) until you see the marked way leading into the grounds of the Scottish National Gallery of Modern Art (see page 35). Once you've explored this gallery and marvelled at the award-winning *Landform Ueda* in the grounds, cross Belford

Road to visit Dean Gallery (see page 35) with its collection of work by Scottish-born Eduardo Paolozzi, said to be the father of pop art. There are excellent café-bars at both galleries.

If you feel you've been on your feet for long enough,

you can take the hourly shuttle bus back to the city centre (ask at the gallery for details). If not, follow Belford Road eastwards until you reach Queensferry, turning left into Randolph Place which brings you into Charlotte Square and the New Town.

OLD TOWN TRAIL

This walk explores parts of the Old Town and the Royal Mile, from the Castle to the Palace of Holyroodhouse, allowing plenty of opportunity for sightseeing on the way.

Start at Edinburgh Castle, spending an hour or so exploring its craggy secrets, if you like. When you leave, walk down Castlehill until you reach The Hub, the Edinburgh Festival Centre, just where the Lawnmarket starts and Johnston Terrace curls round into the Royal Mile. Cut across the front of The Hub (calling in for coffee if it's that time of day) and veer left down Upper Bow. The steps will take you along the top tier of Victoria Street. When you reach the end of

the walkway (where you meet George IV Bridge), do a sharp about-turn to walk down the curving hill at ground level.

At the bottom of Victoria Street, you'll find yourself in the Grassmarket, now full of pleasant shops and cafés but once a notorious den of thieves and place of public execution. After exploring here, head east towards and along Candlemaker Row. You'll see the famous statue of the little terrier Greyfriars Bobby in front of Greyfriars Kirkyard where his master is buried. The churchyard is worth exploring in its own right. Retrace your steps towards the statue and cross over into Chambers

Street where you'll see the Museum of Scotland.

Follow Chambers Street then turn left along South Bridge until you reach the Royal Mile again. The building on your left is Tron Kirk, once a church and now an information centre, exhibition space – and archaeological dig. Here you can see excavations showing part of the old streets. Turn downhill, along the High Street, which turns into Canongate. There's The Netherbow Arts Centre, the Museum of Childhood and The People's Story to explore. On your left is Canongate Kirk with its distinctive red doors.

Look for the alleyway just beyond. Dunbar's Close looks just like any other, but if you walk inside you'll suddenly find yourself in a delightful little garden, a good place for a quiet sit. When you've got your breath back, carry on down Canongate until you see the Scottish Parliament and, just beyond it, the Palace of Holyroodhouse and the Queen's Gallery. They are all well worth visiting – so take your pick.

Dunbar's Close Gardens

THE PALACE OF HOLYROOD-HOUSE

DURBAR'S CLOSE GARDENS

CANONGATE KIRK

THE PEOPLE'S STORY

HORSE WYND

CANONGATE

SCOTTISH PARLIAMENT

MUSEUM OF EDINBURGH

HOLYROOD ROAD

QUEEN'S GALLERY

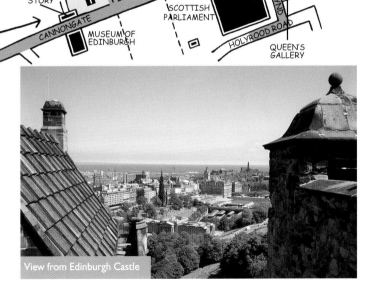
View from Edinburgh Castle

Scott Monument

SIGHTSEEING

Dramatic history, remarkable art, arresting architecture, innovative museums and a world-class botanic garden combine to make Edinburgh a fantastic tourist destination, with more than enough to see and do in fine and (occasionally) foul weather.

The city centre is compact enough to explore on foot, although you might want to hop on a bus to discover the delights of Leith, where the former Royal Yacht *Britannia* is moored and open to visitors.

Brass Rubbing Centre
Trinity Apse, Chalmers Close,
Royal Mile; map F4

This activity centre is inside all that's left of the ancient Trinity College Church, founded nearly 700 years ago. Here are replicas, ranging from ancient Pictish stones to medieval church brasses, which you can rub. You don't need to know how to do it – there's always someone to help. If you prefer to buy one they prepared earlier, that's all right too.

Open: Apr–Sep: Mon–Sat 10.00–17.00; Sun (Aug only) 12.00–17.00
Entry: free (but a charge for making a rubbing)
Tel: 0131 556 4364
Website: www.cac.org.uk
Disabled access: none
Other facilities: shop

Calton Hill
map F2

A climb up the long flight of steps from Waterloo Place brings you to Calton Hill, where you get the best views over the city. You could be forgiven for thinking that this was an abandoned stage set, with so many extraordinary monuments dotted about. The unfinished 'Parthenon' is the National Monument designed by William Playfair to honour those who fell in the Napoleonic Wars but abandoned when funds ran out. Then there's the grandiose Nelson

Nelson Monument

Monument (which you can climb for a small fee) while opposite stands the huge Monument to Dugald Stewart (also by Playfair). Stewart was a professor of philosophy. Two observatories complete the picture. The Royal Observatory, however, is at Blackford Hill on the south side of the city.

Open: Nelson Monument: Apr–Sep: Tue–Sat 10.00–18.00, Mon 13.00–18.00; Oct–Mar: Mon–Sat 10.00–15.00
Entry to Nelson Monument: under £5
Website: www.cac.org.uk
Disabled access: none

Camera Obscura and World of Illusions
Castlehill; map C4

The camera obscura – a dark room where images (in this case views of Edinburgh) are projected onto a flat surface – was installed in the Outlook Tower in this tall building in 1853. It's a good way to introduce yourself to Edinburgh, by watching and listening to a commentary on all you see. They've added a raft of other things to entertain you: a gallery of illusions, a hologram show, images of Victorian Edinburgh and 3D cityscapes. You can climb onto the

Royal Observatory

Camera Obscura

roof and view the goings-on down below through telescopes too.
Open: daily; Apr–June: 9.30–18.00; Jul–Aug: 9.30–19.30; Sep–Oct: 9.30–18.00; Nov–Mar: 10.00–17.00
Entry: under £10
Tel: 0131 226 3709
Website: www.camera-obscura.co.uk
Disabled access: none
Other facilities: shop

Dean Gallery and Scottish National Gallery of Modern Art
Belford Road

Standing on opposite sides of the road, these two galleries have outstanding collections. The Dean is home to the major part of the work of Scottish-born Eduardo Paolozzi, whose distinctive post-modernist sculptures can also be seen in many places in the city. The Gallery of Modern Art has major works by Bacon, Derain, Hirst, Mondrian, Picasso, Matisse, Moore and Whiteread,

as well as works by important Scottish artists including Lambie, Watt and Borland. You can reach the galleries by a pleasant walkway beside the Water of Leith from the city centre, or you could take the free shuttle bus that connects all the Edinburgh galleries.
Open: daily; 10.00–17.00, late night Thu 10.00–19.00
Entry: free (there may be a charge for some temporary exhibitions)
Tel: 0131 624 6200 (infoline 0131 332 2266)
Website: www.nationalgalleries.org
Disabled access: full
Other facilities: shops and cafés

Dynamic Earth
Holyrood Road; map H4

To read about volcanoes, earthquakes, icebergs and the rainforest is one thing; to experience these natural phenomena is another. Almost as realistic is a visit to Dynamic Earth, a Millennium project that has become one of Edinburgh's top attractions. An 18th-century Edinburgh geologist, James Hutton, was the first to gauge the true timescale of Earth's evolution, and it is in tribute to him that this £39 million exhibition centre with its

Dynamic Earth

interactive galleries has been set up at the lower end of Canongate.

Open: Apr–Oct: daily, 10.00–17.00; Jul–Aug: daily, 10.00–18.00; Nov–Mar: Wed–Sun 10.00–17.00

Entry: under £10

Tel: 0131 550 7800

Website: www.dynamicearth.co.uk

Disabled access: full

Other facilities: shop, café, and soft play area for children

Edinburgh Castle

Edinburgh Castle
Castlehill; map B4–C5

The Castle, a fortress on its craggy outcrop, has been the focus for centuries of much of the turbulent history of Scotland. Now tourists come in ever-increasing numbers to marvel at this seemingly impregnable cluster of buildings, approachable only from the east as sheer rock walls forbid any other entry. Mary Queen of Scots and her second husband, Lord Darnley, had their entwined initials engraved above the palace doorway. And in the palace is the tiny room where Mary gave birth to her son James, who was to become king of both England and Scotland.

Here too are the 'Honours', Scotland's crown jewels, the sceptre, the sword and the jewel-encrusted crown made for James V and incorporating the thin gold circlet worn by Robert the Bruce. In the same display is the Stone of Destiny, a chunk of sandstone on which the early kings of Scotland were said to have been crowned. Stolen by the English king Edward I in 1296, it was not restored to Scotland until 1996. Get ready to stick your fingers in your ears at one o'clock when a cannon is fired daily, except on Sundays, from the Castle's Mills Mount battery.

Try to visit the Castle on a fine day – if a 'haar' (a clammy mist) is blowing off the sea, you'll miss the views. You can join a guided tour (included in the entrance fee) or hire an excellent audioguide, which allows you to view at your own pace and inclination.

DON'T MISS

St Margaret's Chapel, the oldest building in the Castle (12th century), dedicated to Queen Margaret, wife of Malcolm III and mother of David I.

Mons Meg, the giant cannon, said to have fired a 500-pound stone nearly two miles (227-kilogram stone just over three kilometres).

The Thin Red Line – the famous painting by Robert Gibb in the National War Museum (in the Castle), showing the 93rd (Highland) Regiment holding their own, although standing only two deep, at the Battle of Balaclava.

Open: daily; Apr–Oct: 9.30–18.00; Nov–Mar: 9.30–17.00
Entry: around £10, audioguides extra
Tel: 0131 225 9846
Website: www.edinburghcastle.biz
Disabled access: limited
Other facilities: café and shop

St Margaret's Chapel window

View from the Castle

The Georgian House

Gladstone's Land

The Georgian House
7 Charlotte Square; map A3

Charlotte Square, designed by Robert Adam just before his death in 1792, is one of the New Town's most successful creations. It is here (at No. 28) that the National Trust for Scotland has its headquarters. Across the way is The Georgian House, also owned by the Trust and partly open to the public. Look for paintings by Ramsay and Raeburn – both Edinburgh men – and enjoy the kitchen and the original wine cellar.

Open: daily; Apr–Oct: 10.00–17.00; Mar and Nov–24 Dec: 11.00–15.00
Entry: around £5
Tel: 0131 225 2160
Website: www.nts.org.uk
Disabled access: limited
Other facilities: gift shop

Gladstone's Land
Lawnmarket; map D4

This tenement house, with its six storeys, once belonged to wealthy merchant Thomas Gledstanes who bought it in 1617 and removed the wooden gallery on the ground floor to create the arcaded stone front. He and his family probably lived on the third floor, renting out the rest. Now it belongs to the National Trust for Scotland and you can visit the first two floors. The Trust has recreated a 17th-century shopping booth and restored the remaining rooms – one with an impressive painted ceiling – in authentic period style. If you really want to get a feel for the place, you can stay here – but you'll have to book well in advance. See page 93 for details of how to book the apartment.

Open: daily; Apr–end Oct: Mon–Sat 10.00–17.00, Sun 14.00–17.00
Entry: around £5
Tel: 0131 226 5856
Website: www.nts.org.uk
Disabled access: limited
Other facilities: gift shop

Greyfriars Bobby
Candlemaker Row;
map D5

If you're of a senti-
mental disposition,
take a hanky with
you when you go
to see the world-
famous statue of this
faithful little dog.
Bobby, a perky Skye
terrier, worked with
his master, police-
man John Gray, who
died in 1858. Gray

Greyfriars Bobby

was buried at Greyfriars Kirk in the Old
Town and his dog began what was to
become a 14-year vigil over his beloved
master's grave. He was looked after by
the people of Edinburgh and the statue,
made while he was still alive, was put up
when he died and he was at last
reunited with his master.

Greyfriars Kirkyard
off Candlemaker Row; map D5

Many Edinburgh notables are buried
here, although it is mostly visited for its
associations with Greyfriars Bobby. Here
is the magnificent tomb dedicated to
the 18th-century architects, the Adams.
Another architect, James Craig, designer
of the New Town street layout, is here
too, along with poet and novelist Allan
Ramsay (father of the painter). But
Greyfriars Kirkyard is also remembered
as the place where in 1638 Scottish
nobles, ministers and about 5,000
ordinary people lined up to sign the
National Covenant, opposing Charles I's
attempts to impose both the English
prayer book in Scottish churches and
bishops in the Scottish parliament.
There is a memorial to the Covenanters
who were imprisoned here in 1679 for
their stand for political independence
and for Presbyterianism.

Greyfriars Kirkyard

Heart of Midlothian

Heart of Midlothian
High Street, map D4

You'll notice this heart-shaped arrangement of bricks outside St Giles' Cathedral. It marks the site of the now-demolished Tolbooth, which jutted out into the street and served as the civic centre. Sir Walter Scott's novel *The Heart of Midlothian* gave the building this name. Be careful where you tread – many passers-by spit on the 'heart' for luck.

The High Kirk of St Giles
Parliament Square, Royal Mile; map D4/5

Although St Giles is often called a 'cathedral', it is not the seat of a bishop. Inside you'll see a statue of Protestant reformer John Knox who led his crusade for Scottish Presbyterianism from the pulpit here. The present church, with its four massive piers supporting the tower, dates mainly from the late 15th century but to a 19th-century redesign. In the north aisle you'll see windows designed by William Morris and Edward Burne-Jones; close by is one dedicated to Robert Burns. Robert Louis Stevenson reclines on a chaise longue in a bronze relief. The story goes that the original piece of work by American artist Augustus St Gaudens had him lounging

HIDDEN HISTORY

Tiny Tron Kirk on the corner of the High Street and South Bridge on the Royal Mile (map E4) is now an Information Centre that offers a deep insight into Edinburgh's past. Inside you can walk round excavations revealing parts of Marlin's Wynd, an old close which once housed a market and bookshops. You'll also find an exhibition on the history of the Old Town inside the old church.

The High Kirk of St Giles

on a bed smoking a cigarette. That one had to be re-thought.

DON'T MISS

The extraordinary Chapel of the Order of the Thistle with its wonderful carved interior. You'll even see an angel playing bagpipes. The chapel, modelled on St George's Chapel, Windsor, was built in 1911 by Robert Lorimer for the 16 Knights of the Order of the Thistle.
Open: daily; May–Sep: Mon–Fri 9.00–19.00, Sat 9.00–17.00, Sun 13.00–17.00; Oct–Apr: Mon–Sat 9.00–17.00, Sun 13.00–17.00
Entry: free (a donation of at least £1 is suggested)
Tel: 0131 225 9442
Website: www.stgilescathedral.org.uk
Disabled access: full
Other facilities: shop and café

Jenners

48 Princes Street; map D3
Before you step inside the marble, carved wood and galleried interior of Edinburgh's best-loved store (and you surely will), glance up at the ornate exterior. Female figures or caryatides, appearing to bear the weight of the upper storeys, are a tribute to the role of women in supporting this, the world's oldest independent department store. When colleagues Charles Kennington and Charles Jenner were sacked from their jobs in 1838 for slipping off to Musselburgh Races, they set up their drapery, promising to provide 'every prevailing British and Parisian fashion in silks, shawls, fancy dresses, ribbons, lace, hosiery'. They were true to their word.

More than 170 years later, Jenners is still a leader in the fashion stakes. Today's building, designed by William Hamilton Beattie in 1893, was in its day a miracle of modernity, with lavish electric lighting, lifts, air conditioning and elegant balconies. It is a pleasure to explore.
Open: daily; Mon, Wed, Fri, Sat 9.00–18.00, Tue 9.30–18.00, Thu 9.00–20.00, Sun 11.00–17.00
Website: www.jenners.com
Disabled access: full
Other facilities: café

Jenners

John Knox's House
High Street, Royal Mile; map F4

This much-photographed, three-storeyed building jutting out into the High Street was probably lived in only briefly by Calvinist John Knox, although the museum inside will give you a good idea of his life and work. We do know though that the house was owned by goldsmith James Mosman, jeweller to Mary Queen of Scots, and there's a recreation of a goldsmith's studio here too. The 15th/16th century building has been closed for refurbishment and should re-open by spring 2005.

Open: Mon–Sat 10.00–17.00
Entry: under £5
Tel: 0131 556 9579
Website: www.scottishstorytellingcentre.co.uk
Disabled access: limited
Other facilities: shop

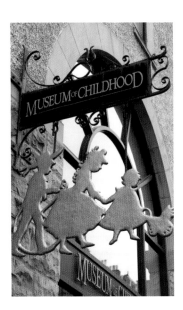

OFF THE WALL
You might be in Edinburgh when the Mansfield Traquair Centre has an open day to show off the murals painted here in the last decade of the 19th century by Edinburgh Arts and Crafts artist Phoebe Anna Traquair. The former Catholic Apostolic church at Mansfield Place, at the foot of Broughton Street, has been converted into a function space and the murals are on display on certain days. Their website is www.mansfieldtraquair.org.uk.

Museum of Childhood
42 High Street, Royal Mile; map F4

This jolly space is packed with parents and their children, all enjoying themselves. It's as much a history lesson as a series of galleries full of books, toys, teddy bears, games and puzzles. Adults like the nostalgic trip to the toys of their own past while youngsters are delighted to see the games young people played and the toys that endure.

Open: Mon–Sat 10.00–17.00; Sun (Jul–Aug only) 12.00–17.00; last admission 16.45
Entry: free
Tel: 0131 529 4142
Website: www.cac.org.uk
Disabled access: limited
Other facilities: shop

The Museum of Edinburgh
142 Canongate, Royal Mile; map G3

If you want to see Greyfriars Bobby's collar and bowl, this is the place to find them. The museum has a large collection of material relating to the city, some beautiful silver and glass and, most important of all, the original National Covenant of 1638. Huntly House, where the treasures are displayed, was built in the 16th century.

Open: Mon–Sat 10.00–17.00, Sun (Aug only) 12.00–17.00
Entry: free
Tel: 0131 529 4143
Website: www.cac.org.uk
Disabled access: full

Museum of Scotland
Chambers Street; map E5

If you visit here hungry for knowledge about Scotland, its culture, people, traditions and the land itself, you'll go away entirely satisfied – and probably come back for a second helping. This beautiful new building (opened in 1998) of sandstone quarried from the hills near Elgin is entered through a rounded tower, into a terrific series of exhibition spaces. Make for the information desk in the central atrium and get your bearings before starting the exploration of Scotland from its origins.

Begin by looking at Scotland's (and Europe's) oldest rock, a chunk of Lewisian gneiss, to give a sense of the immense timescale. Distinctive bronze sculptures each contain glass-fronted cases displaying early necklaces, bracelets, pins, brooches and torques. There are treasure hoards, too, and a most beautiful installation from artist Andrew Goldsworthy of four high, perfectly curved walls made from painstakingly stacked slate. The same artist has also arranged a complete whale skeleton into a perfect round. As you work your way up from floor to floor, you'll encounter the full story of Scotland's history, its industry and the achievements of Scottish people, both inside their own country and worldwide. The top floor contains an unexpected display of objects chosen by Scots to mark the 20th century. And it doesn't stop here – a lift will take you to the roof garden where you can gaze across to the Firth of Forth and the Castle.

DON'T MISS

Eduardo Paolozzi's distinctive figurative bronze sculptures that contain the glass-fronted display cases.
The famous Lewis chessmen, carved from walrus tusks.
Open: daily: Mon 10.00–17.00, Tue 10.00–20.00, Wed–Sat 10.00–17.00, Sun 12.00–17.00
Entry: free
Tel: 0131 247 4422
Website: www.nms.ac.uk
Disabled access: full
Other facilities: restaurant, shop and children's discovery centre

National Gallery of Scotland
The Mound; map C4

The joy of a visit to this imposing gallery with its outstanding works of art is the arrangement of the paintings in smallish rooms, allowing you to absorb them in a manageable way. On the main floor, the collection of 16th-century Italian paintings include Raphael's *Bridgewater Madonna* and *The Holy Family with a Palm Tree*, the latter now brilliantly restored. Titian's works include the tender and sensuous *Three Ages of Man*. On this floor, in a room of their own, you'll find Poussin's *Seven Sacraments,* the artist's innovative portrayals of Jesus and early members of the Christian Church.

Upstairs there's an equally good collection of French Impressionists. The gallery's most famous work of art, *The Three Graces* by Canova, is on loan to London's Victoria and Albert Museum until 2006. On the lower floor is a comprehensive collection of works of Scottish painters, including Raeburn, Ramsay, William McTaggart and Sir David Wilkie. For one month, in January when the weak light will do the least damage, the Gallery's collection of Turner watercolours can be seen.

DON'T MISS
Rembrandt's wonderful painting *Woman in Bed*, thought to represent Sarah on her wedding night, waiting for her husband, Tobias, to chase away the devil.
Open: daily; Mon–Wed 10.00–17.00, Thu 10.00–19.00, Fri–Sun 10.00–17.00
Entry: free (there may be a charge for special exhibitions)

Tel: 0131 624 6200 (infoline 0131 332 2266)
Website: www.nationalgalleries.org
Disabled access: full
Other facilities: shop

National War Museum of Scotland
Edinburgh Castle; map C5

This six-roomed museum focuses on the lives of Scottish soldiers, the weapons they used and their experience of battle. So we have eve-of-battle letters such as this from 2nd Lieutenant William Paterson to his parents: '… I feel it my duty to write you this last message of love, which will only reach you in the event of my death. The fact is, we are on the eve of a great battle of advance, and with my platoon, I have been detailed to go to the furthest objective, 3,500 yards from the trenches …'. Paterson was killed in action on 20 November 1917.

There is a locket with hair belonging to Sir John Moore, immortalized after his burial at Corunna in the poem by Wolfe ('Not a drum was heard, not a funeral note …'). There are the usual uniforms, medals and paintings of daring deeds, too. Separate exhibitions in Edinburgh Castle show the traditions of the Royal Scots and the Scots Dragoon Guards.
Open: daily; Apr–Oct: 9.45–17.45; Nov–Mar: 9.45–16.45
Entry: included in entry for Edinburgh Castle (see page 37)
Tel: 0131 225 7534
Website: www.nms.ac.uk
Disabled access: full
Other facilities: shop, and café (in the Castle)

Holyrood Abbey ruins

State apartments

The Palace of Holyroodhouse and the Queen's Gallery
Holyrood Road, map H3

Legend has it that King David I, out hunting, was unseated by a magnificent stag which made as if to gore him. In desperation the king clutched at its huge antlers and found himself holding a rood, or holy cross. That night, in a dream, he was commanded to built a house 'devoted to the Cross'. Thus came about Holyrood Abbey; the Palace grew up later, on the site of the Abbey guest house. It seemed much more comfortable, tucked away in a sheltered spot at the end of the Royal Mile, than the often bleak Castle. James II was the first Scottish king to build a wing here for the exclusive use of the monarchy, while James IV topped that with a proper palace. Not to be outdone, Charles II (who never lived in Holyrood) rebuilt most of what we see today.

You'll see not only the state apartments (where the Queen appointed the late Donald Dewar the new First Minister of Scotland in May 1999) but also the older historical apartments. Here is the tiny room where the jealous Lord Darnley, husband to Mary Queen of Scots, organized the brutal and fatal stabbing of David Rizzio as he sat with the queen and her ladies, playing cards. The Queen's Bedchamber is a small room – almost too compact for the 1.8-metre (6-foot) tall queen. Next door in the Outer Chamber there is a good display of needlework made by Mary during her long captivity, paintings and other royal mementos. Downstairs in the Great Gallery you might be bemused by portraits of very early Scottish royals. As no one knew what they looked like when the paintings were commissioned from Dutch artist Jacob de Wet, he had to use his imagination, which was clearly limited; they all have the same long-nosed face. This is still a royal residence, so public access varies. Check before you visit.

The Queen's Gallery, built inside the environs of the Palace, can be visited separately, although you'll get a reduction for a combined ticket. The Gallery is worth visiting simply for the quality of the craftsmanship of the building. Opened in 2002 to celebrate the Queen's Golden Jubilee, the space was created where the old Holyrood Free Church and the Duchess of Gordon's School once stood. Now there's a new arched entrance, built of stone and glorious with Scotland's lion prominent. The arch is decorated with a carved garland of wild flowers, while the hinges of the entrance doors are shaped as boughs of native trees – chestnut, laburnum, oak, rowan and hawthorn. If you walk past at night you'll see it reflected by lights set into the paving. An inner screen, with sculpted figures as 'handles', takes you into the gallery itself with its wonderful native timber staircase curving away to the upper level. The Gallery shows paintings from the Royal Collection.

DON'T MISS

The miniature portrait of Mary Queen of Scots by François Clouet.

The Darnley Jewel – a magnificent heart-shaped jewel, richly enamelled, full of family symbolism. Kept for a long time in the library at Windsor Palace, it's now on display at Holyrood.

The interactive display at the Queen's Gallery, allowing you to see the whole Royal Collection on screen.

Open: daily; Apr–end Oct: 9.30–18.00; Nov–end Mar: 9.30–16.30; Palace or Gallery may close during these times – check before you visit

> **T ELLING STORIES**
> The Netherbow on the Royal Mile, exactly halfway between Edinburgh Castle and the Palace of Holyroodhouse, used to be one of the principal gates of the city. Now it's home to the Scottish Storytelling Centre with a new 100-seat theatre and interactive storytelling space, which should be open from autumn 2005.

Entry: Palace, under £10; Queen's Gallery, under £5; combined ticket, under £15

Tel: 0131 556 5100

Website: www.royal.gov.uk and follow links to royal residences

Disabled access: limited

Other facilities: shop and tea room

Holyrood Palace

The People's Story
Canongate Tolbooth, Canongate; map G3

The Tolbooth, next to Canongate Kirk, has been used variously as local government offices and a prison. Now it tells the story of the ordinary people of the city over the last 200 years and it does it well. 'The High Street in Edinburgh is inhabited by a greater number of persons than any other street in Europe,' commented Edward Topham in 1774. He was referring to Edinburgh Old Town, where tenement lifestyle meant that the poor lived right at the top of the high buildings or at the very bottom. The well-to-do enjoyed a more comfortable lifestyle somewhere in the middle. This exhibition shows you how that worked and uses sounds, tableaux and display material to recreate a prison cell, a reform parade, workshops, a wartime kitchen and much else besides, including engaging scenes in a teashop and a pub where husbands and wives discuss each other and the prospects of a match between Hibs (Hiberian FC) and the 'jam tarts' (Hearts).

Open: Mon–Sat 10.00–17.00; Sun during the Festival 14.00–17.00
Entry: free
Tel: 0131 529 4057
Website: www.edinburgh.gov.uk (and follow links)
Disabled access: limited
Other facilities: shop

Royal Botanic Garden
Inverleith Row

Even if you're not into plants, you'll enjoy the lovely setting on a hillside with views over the city. From spring, when the rhododendrons and azaleas set the grounds ablaze with colour, to summer, when the enormous herbaceous border comes into its own, and to autumn with its rich and mellow tones, this is a garden for all seasons. The alpine beds and houses are not to be missed – nor are the glasshouses which take you on a trip through the regions of the world and their rich and varied flora. If you're staying in or near the city centre, the garden is a 20-minute stroll through some interesting New Town streets.

Open: daily; 10.00–between 16.00 and 19.00 depending on season
Entry: free although there is a charge (under £5) for entry to the glasshouses
Tel: 0131 552 7171
Website: www.rbge.org.uk
Disabled access: full
Other facilities: café, gift shop, exhibitions in the hall and in Inverleith House gallery, plants for sale

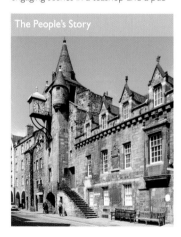

The People's Story

Royal Botanic Garden

Detail of gate

Royal Museum
Chambers Street; map E5

This is a complete contrast to the adjoining Museum of Scotland (see pages 43–44) and just as delightful. The airy Victorian building, elegant with built-in fishponds and fountains, glass and wrought iron, contains 36 galleries housing international collections of decorative arts, science, archaeology, the natural world and industry.

Perhaps the greatest draw is the Millennium Clock, in the main hall. At set times crowds gather round it to see the strange carved figures 'perform' as the clock strikes. Downstairs, too, you can't fail to see the giant totem pole from British Columbia and sculpture from Rome, Greece and Nubia. There's a beam engine designed by James Watt and a control desk from Hunterston A nuclear reactor. Upstairs, a wander through the galleries will give you mummies from Egypt, enamels, silver-ware, jewellery, woodcarving and costumes from Europe, and pots from ancient Greece.

DON'T MISS
The Millennium Clock, made by six craftsmen and women to mark the new century, a strangely attractive neo-Gothic creation, full of allegory.
The gift shop, shared with the adjoining National Museum, where you can buy the most attractive presents, all related to items in the two museums.
Open: daily; Mon 10.00–17.00, Tue 10.00–20.00, Wed–Sat 10.00–17.00, Sun 12.00–17.00

Millennium Clock, Royal Museum

Entry: free (there is a charge for some of the visiting exhibitions)
Tel: 0131 247 4422
Website: www.nms.ac.uk
Disabled access: full
Other facilities: café and shop

Royal Scottish Academy building
The Mound; map C3

William Playfair's elaborate Grecian-style building with Queen Victoria and a pair of sphinxes sitting aloft has undergone an extensive renovation to link it with the nearby National Gallery, both physically and in the exhibitions it shows.
Open: daily; Fri–Wed 10.00–17.00; Thu 10.00–19.00
Entry: free (there may be a charge for special exhibitions)
Tel: 0131 624 6200 (infoline 0131 332 2266)
Website: www.nationalgalleries.org
Disabled access: full
Other facilities: shop

MONUMENTAL ANGELS

If you enjoy Victoriana, you really ought to pay a visit to Dean Cemetery, alongside the Dean Gallery and accessible from the Water of Leith Walkway. It's crammed full of the most incredible monuments, ornate tombstones, carved angels, obelisks and memorial pyramids.

IN LOVING MEMORY
OF
GEORGE DALZIEL

The Royal Yacht Britannia

The Royal Yacht Britannia
Ocean Terminal, Leith

For 44 years *Britannia* sailed more than 1,600,000 kilometres (1,000,000 miles) in the service of the Royal Family. Now owned by a charitable trust, she's one of Edinburgh's top tourist attractions. There are plenty of buses going to the Ocean Terminal (look for No. 22 at the top of Princes Street or from Leith Walk), but it's best to ring ahead to book for *Britannia* as access is limited. Once aboard you'll find the surroundings less glamorous than you expected.
Open: daily; Apr–Sep: 9.30–16.30; Oct–Mar: 10.00–15.30
Entry: under £10
Tel: 0131 555 5566
Website: www.royalyachtbritannia.co.uk
Disabled access: full
Other facilities: shop

Scotch Whisky Heritage Centre
Castlehill, Royal Mile; map C5

If it's a dreich day when you visit the Castle it might be an idea to call in here to get an insight (and a taste) of Scotland's favourite refreshment. You'll see how it's made, meet a ghost, have a ride in a barrel and learn a lot about the art of blending whisky. A free dram is included in the tour price and, if you like what you taste, the shop is stacked from floor to ceiling with a huge range of different brands.
Open: daily; May–Sep: 9.30–18.30; Oct–Apr: 10.00–18.00
Entry: full tour: under £10; barrel-ride only: around £5
Tel: 0131 220 0441
Website: www.whisky-heritage.co.uk
Disabled access: full
Other facilities: shop

Scott Monument
Princes Street; map D3

You need to have a good head for heights to climb the winding stairs inside this amazing 183-metre (200-foot) structure, built to honour the writer Sir Walter Scott. The dark monument itself is an insight into Scott's work, with statuettes of his characters built into it. The great man himself, with his favourite deerhound Maida, sits inside, carved from a huge block of marble. It is said to be the largest memorial in the world to a writer.
Open: daily; Apr–Sep: Mon–Sat 9.00–18.00, Sun 10.00–18.00; Oct–Mar: Mon–Sat 9.00–15.00, Sun 10.00–15.00
Entry: under £5
Tel: 0131 529 4068
Website: www.cac.org.uk

Scottish National Portrait Gallery
Queen Street, Edinburgh; map D2

Even before you start looking at paintings, you'll enjoy the ornate Gothic sandstone exterior of this building, said to be modelled by architect Sir Robert Rowland Anderson on the Doge's Palace in Venice. Once inside, you're distracted again by the remarkable murals painted by William Hole. There's a frieze showing famous Scots (and there are lots of them) and, above this, the battles of Bannockburn and Largs and other defining scenes from Scottish history. If you climb up to the balcony, you'll enjoy the sculpted busts on each staircase. The permanent collection on the upper floors is another slice of Scottish history, told by its people. The exhibitions on the ground floor, which houses the café (best scones in the city, say some) and shop, change regularly.

Open: daily; 10.00–17.00, late night Thu 10.00–19.00
Entry: free
Tel: 0131 624 6200 (infoline 0131 332 2266)

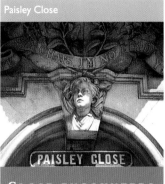
Paisley Close

PAISLEY CLOSE

CLOSE ENCOUNTERS
Among the closes and wynds (small courtyards) of the Royal Mile you'll see Paisley Close with its bust of a young man above the entrance and the inscription 'Heave awa' chaps, I'm no dead yet'. This refers to the rescue of a young lad in 1861 when the tenement collapsed and rescuers were sifting through the rubble.

Website: www.nationalgalleries.org
Disabled access: full
Other facilities: shop and café

Scottish Parliament
Horsewynd; map H3

The new £431-million building – planned to resemble a harbour scene of upturned boats – was officially opened in October 2004, £391 million over budget and three years behind schedule. The controversial building was designed by Enric Miralles, the Catalan architect who

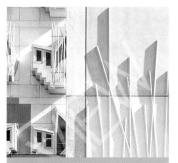
Scottish Parliament

Scottish National Portrait Gallery

died in 2000, two years after he won the design contract.

Open: daily; Tue–Thu 9.00–19.00, Sat–Sun 10.00–16.00, Fri & Mon (Apr–Oct) 10.00–18.00, (Nov–Mar) 10.00–16.00
Entry: free (guided tours under £5)
Tel: 0131 384 5000
Website: www.scottish.parliament.uk
Disabled access: full
Other facilities: shop and café

The Writers' Museum
Lady Stair's Close, Lawnmarket; map D4

Lady Stair was the glorious but far from strait-laced society hostess on whom Sir Walter Scott based his story *My Aunt Margaret's Mirror,* so it is fitting that the museum devoted to the works of Scott, Burns and Robert Louis Stevenson should be in her former house. Here you'll find personal bits and pieces of each of these three, including Scott's chessboard, Burns's desk and the press used to print the Waverley novels. Temporary exhibitions feature the lives and work of other Scottish writers.

Open: daily; Mon–Sat 10.00–17.00, Sun (Aug only) 12.00–17.00
Entry: free
Tel: 0131 529 4901
Website: www.cac.org.uk
Disabled access: none

The Writers' Museum

TREAT YOURSELF
Visit Valvona and Crolla in Leith Walk, the city's much valued Italian/Scottish deli and enjoy coffee, tea or lunch in their café behind the well-stocked shelves of the shop.

Sculpture in Leith Walk

BREATHING SPACE

Even in the heart of the city you're never far away from a green and leafy space. Princes Street, one of the busiest shopping areas in the country, has commercial premises on one side only – the other side slopes away to sunken gardens which afford distant views across to the Castle and the Old Town.

Princes Street Gardens;
map A4–D3
These spacious and well-laid-out gardens were formed when the boggy Nor' Loch was drained and filled in when the New Town was built. Now there are paths, trees and colourful flowerbeds with plenty of places to sit, read, relax and picnic. You can enter the gardens from Princes Street, The Mound or from Market Street.

Dunbar's Close Gardens;
map G3
Just off the Royal Mile, through an ancient arch-

Princes Street Gardens

way, you'll find one of Edinburgh's secret places. Next to Canongate Kirk is Dunbar's Close, a peaceful walled garden, bounded by tall tenements. There are borders backed by trimmed yew hedges, a knot garden, tidy pathways and places to sit.

Museum of Scotland roof garden;
map E5
If you want to hit the heights, take the lift up to the often forgotten roof garden on top of this award-winning museum. You'll be rewarded with sweeping views over the

Holyrood Park

city and across to the Pentland Hills and the Firth of Forth.

Holyrood Park; map H4–H5

Just a few steps off the city streets and suddenly you're in a real Scottish landscape – craggy outcrops, hills, moorland, lochs; it seems all of Scotland is here. Take a picnic or just a walk. If you're feeling energetic you could aim for Arthur's Seat, a towering extinct volcano which reaches 254 metres (832 feet) above sea level, giving tremendous views across

the city. There are several entrances to the park, the most obvious being by the Palace of Holyroodhouse.

Royal Botanic Garden; Inverleith Row

The stroll out to these wonderful gardens is itself a pleasure through the elegant New Town. Entry is free (see page 48 for more details and opening times) and you're welcome to take a picnic.

Calton Hill; map F2

Take the steps from Waterloo Place at the end of Princes Street for a

climb up to this extraordinary monument-littered hill. There's plenty of space here though and wonderful views of both the Castle and Arthur's Seat.

St Margaret's Loch, Holyrood Park

SHOPPING

Bill Baber (page 64)

If you enjoy the thrill of finding enticing shops off the main drag, Edinburgh is the city for you. Stroll along the atmospheric Royal Mile in the Old Town – the smaller streets here are full of interesting, independently owned shops.

Three Estaits, the Randolph Gallery, the Edinburgh Gallery, Unicorn Antiques, The Dundas Street Gallery, The Scottish Gallery – and many more.

Princes Street, for all its grandeur, is – with one notable exception – crammed with High Street chain stores. The exception is Jenners, the world's oldest independent department store, glorious in its architecture – as exclusive as Harrods in London and Saks Fifth Avenue in New York.

Victoria Street; map D5

The Red Door Gallery has much to interest art lovers, while Murdoch McLeod at Bow Well Antiques and Jewellery specializes in all things Scottish, from ancient curling stones to an enormous stuffed elk.

Shopping hours are generally 9.00–17.30 Monday to Saturday, with many shops opening later and closing earlier on Sunday. Many of the larger shops stay open late on Thursday evening.

High Street stores

Apart from the stores in Princes Street itself there are two shopping centres nearby. Next door to Waverley Station is the glossy, underground Princes Mall shopping centre with its attractive marbled piazza at street level, while more chain stores, including a huge

John Lewis, occupy St James Centre behind Register House at the eastern (Calton Hill) end of Princes Street.

Art galleries and antique shops

Just take a walk down Dundas Street, which is packed with galleries and salerooms. In the Old Town, the Grassmarket area is a happy hunting ground. Some shops are listed below – but you'll find plenty of others.

Dundas Street; map D1

Take your pick from The

Bow Well Antiques

Old Town Bookshop

Books, maps and prints

There are branches of Waterstones along Princes Street and a well-stocked Ottakars in nearby George Street. Explore the Grassmarket area for a choice of second-hand bookshops.

Broughton Street; map E1

Broughton Books sells a good selection of second-hand hardbacks and paperbacks too.

Canongate; map F4

The Old Children's Bookshelf stocks annuals, pop-up cut-out theatres and the books of your childhood. Nearby is Carson Clark, stuffed full of fascinating old prints, maps, etchings and globes.

Howard Place

Second Edition is located at No. 9 – just across the street from the house where Robert Louis Stevenson was born.

Leith Walk; map F1

McNaughtan's Bookshop, in Haddington Place, just off the main thoroughfare, specializes in art, history, Scottish subjects and the classics as well.

N.W. Circus, Stockbridge

The Stockbridge Bookshop is always a good place for a browse.

Tanfield, Inverleith Row

Aurora Books and Duncan and Reid, which sells antiques as well as books, sit happily next door to each other.

Victoria Street; map D5

The Old Town Bookshop is full of good condition, second-hand books and some very fine prints.

Old Children's Bookshelf

Children's clothes
Broughton Street; map E1
Visit Gertrude and Lily with their pretty clothes for children and some unusual accessories.

Fashion
Edinburgh women – and men – should be among the best dressed in the world: there's no shortage of shops selling clothes from the classic to the frankly funky.

Canongate, The Royal Mile; map F4–H3

Gertrude and Lily

On this, the lower end of the Royal Mile, you'll find Koshka Knitwear – a stitch above the usual designs for sale. All the jumpers and cardigans are hand-framed in Edinburgh. Nearby is Frontiers selling lovely bags, wispy scarves, jewellery and knitwear. More knits at Ragamuffin, on the corner of Canongate and St Mary's Street. They specialize in Isle of Skye jumpers in soft colours. If you really want to look the part, order a kilt in a tartan such as 'Ancient Scotland the Brave' from traditional outfitter Nicolson. They'll supply a matching 'tie scrunch' (neckwear), too.

Forth Street; map E1
Lorraine Wesley sells exclusive designs in this small street just off Broughton Street.

George Street; map B3–C3
This is the street to look for a special outfit: here are Viyella, Jaegar, Jones (shoes), Hobbs, Phase Eight, Escada and Karen Millen. Coast sells exciting clothes while the best-

Nicolson

dressed gents might make a beeline for Crombie. Jackpot, Cruise (for men), Hugo Boss and Gant are all here too. You'll find way-out accessories at The Craze. Turn down Castle Street to find Cruise for women.

Livi

Jeffrey Street; map F4

Here in the Old Town is Livi, with exceptionally pretty clothes, and award-winning Corniche, which stocks designers such as Betsey Johnson, Jean Paul Gaultier and Holly Campbell Mitchell. Chi has inviting designs, and look for Carina Shoes with its beautiful footwear and exciting handbags, too.

Princes Street; map D3

Although it's not the easiest store to navigate, Jenners is certainly one of the most elegant and interesting; look for the Fashion Lab here selling Armani, Versace and DKNY. There's Liz Claiborne, Marella, Nicole Farhi and Joseph among many other labels on the first floor balcony. Further along Princes Street is the old-established Romanes and Paterson, selling tartans, cashmere and Scottish gifts.

Rose Street; map B3–D3

The search for a really special pair of shoes should end at Rogerson Fine Footwear, with a selection of original designs.

St Stephen Street, Stockbridge

Stockbridge is worth visit-

No. 55 St Stephen Street

ing for its village atmosphere and unusual shops. In St Stephen Street you'll find knitwear at No. 2 and retro gear at No. 55.

Teviot Place

Just south of George IV Bridge (map D5). The Rusty Zip has funky retro gear – you can't miss the blue shopfront.

Grassmarket; map C5–D5

The historic Grassmarket has lots of shops to explore. Hawick Cashmere Company sells just that, while the long-established W. Armstrong and Son is where you can look for gear for that retro party – Levis, feather boas, psychedelic shirts and suede shoes.

TREAT YOURSELF

It's little more than a 15-minute walk from the centre of town to the old community of Stockbridge where you'll find a lively mix of shops, cafés and pubs, and a village atmosphere quite different from that of the city itself. The original timber bridge crossing the Water of Leith was known as a 'stock footbridge', hence the name of the area.

W. Armstrong (page 62)

Jane Davidson

Bill Baber

The Walk, St Andrew Square; map D2
You can't miss the large Harvey Nicols with acres of plate glass. Armani and Louis Vuitton complete the upmarket feel while other shops are being attracted to this fairly new development.

Thistle Street; map C2
Jane Davidson will entice you in with displays of Chine silk dresses, Louis Feraud jackets and Jimmy Choo shoes.

Victoria Street; map D5
It's a treat to visit this picturesque area in the Old Town. As you walk down the curved hill you'll see Odd One Out and

Walker Slater selling women's and men's clothes respectively, while Swish sells young fashion. Beautiful knitwear is to be had at Bill Baber. Across the street (confusingly called West Bow) there's Big Ideas, which you may need to visit after a few too many deep-fried Mars Bars. Here too is Byzantium, a collective with stalls selling not only clothes but also jewellery and antiques.

Food and drink
Whisky is the water of life in Scotland and you'll find plenty of touristy and not-so-touristy shops stocking hundreds of different brands. You can also buy

Walker Slater

S O M E T H I N G   D I F F E R E N T
Traditional pubs serve haggis with neeps
(mashed turnips or swede) and tatties
(potatoes) while grander restaurants
combine it with whisky and peppercorns as
a special stuffing. A word of warning – you
can try the deep-fried Mars Bars, served up
in chippies, but it's probably best not to.

haggis (normally made by
MacSween who are based
south of Edinburgh at
Loanhead) and some
other surprising treats to
take home with you.

Broughton Street; map E1
'You can live without
Crombie's sausages – but
what a life!' was the adver-
tising slogan coined in
1955 for Edinburgh's

favourite banger – and it
holds true today. In the
lower half of interesting
Broughton Street you'll
find family butcher's
Crombie's, liked for their
local organic meat but also
for their huge range of
speciality sausages, from
the exotic mango and
apple to delicious chunky
pork. Walk up the hill and
there is the wonderful
Real Foods, chock full of

Crombie's

Real Foods

Demijohn

Moniack
Mead
14.6%

Nordic Vintage Gin
500ml

organic fruit and vege-
tables, dried pulses, fruits,
cereals, spices and a lot
more beside.

Canonmills
There are plenty of good
delicatessens dotted
around the city, but here,
close to Broughton Street,
you'll find two in particular
– the Olive Branch and
the enormous Dionika.

Elm Row, Leith Walk;
map F1
You won't believe that so
much could be crammed
into one shop – and it's
a roomy establishment.
Valvona and Crolla, the
Scottish-Italian deli established more than 90 years
ago, is beloved by locals
and visitors alike. Call in
and you'll see why.

St Mary's Street; map F4
If you long for orange
fizzies, humbugs, Edinburgh
rock, Granny's sookers
or home-made tablet
(fudge), visit Casey's
where the jars of sweets
will take you back to the
days of your childhood.

The Royal Mile;
map D4–H4
There are plenty of whisky
shops but two in the Old

Iain Mellis

Town are particularly
worth visiting. At the
lower end of the Royal
Mile in Canongate is
Cadenhead's, established
in 1862, while Royal Mile
Whiskies is near the
Castle in the High Street.
You'll find the House
of Edin fudge shop in
Canongate and choco-
holics can make a beeline
for Plaisir du Chocolat for
their daily fix.

Victoria Street; map D5
Iain Mellis sells cheese so
good it's worth walking a
long way for – and you'll
leave with more than you
went in for. There are also
branches in Bakers Place,
Stockbridge and
Bruntsfield Place. Next
door to the Victoria Street

Ye Olde Christmas Shoppe

shop is the unique
Demijohn, who have sour-
ced locally made liqueurs
(try the blaeberry or the
cranberry and raspberry),
fruity olive oils, vinegars,
cask-aged malt whiskies
and vintage gin. You taste,
and select an empty bottle
to be filled with whichever
liquid you desire.

Jewellery, gifts – and
some oddities
The oddities come in the
shape of Christmas shops
that are open all year
round. There are three in
the Old Town – two (Ye
Olde Christmas Shoppe
and The Nutcracker) on
The Royal Mile and one at
West Bow on the way
down Victoria Street to
the Grassmarket.

Fioritalia

Halibut and Herring

Bagpipes Galore

of household ware — mugs, bowls, jugs, plates and eggcups.

Frederick Street; map C3
L'Occitane en Provence is well known for its must-have bath-time goodies.

Hanover Street; map C3
Penhaligon's sells soaps, scents and all sorts of delicious-smelling gifts.

Canongate; map G3
Always longed to own a set of bagpipes? Visit Bagpipes Galore and indulge yourself.

High Street; map E4
How about a tartan deckchair? Anta is the place for heathery tartans — ties, rugs, scarves, mugs, bowls and all sorts of other household gifts.

Dundas Street; map C1
The Scottish Gallery is a showcase for quality contemporary Scottish art. Nearby Bridgewater Pottery sells a good range

North Bank Street; map D4
Just Scottish sells really lovely paintings, sculpture,

L'Occitane en Provence

Penhaligon's

jewellery, pottery and prints – not a tartan Scottie dog in sight.

Rodney Street
Fioritalia, near Broughton Street, is one of the city's many flower shops.

Rose Street; map B3
Palenque is here with silver jewellery and original designs incorporating rose quartz and enamel.

St Stephen Street, Stockbridge
Here you'll find Rosie Brown, selling good jewellery and gifts, and the Gramophone Emporium.

Thistle Street; map C2
Antique and period jewellery – very collectable – at Joseph Bonner.

Victoria Street; map D5
Here you'll find Pine and Old Lace – selling Victorian and Edwardian linen and lace – and an interesting bathroom accessory shop called Halibut and Herring. Clarkson sells beautifully designed jewellery, while Costume Ha Ha is the place if you're invited to a fancy dress party and need a costume.

Anta

EATING AND DRINKING

Café culture has come to Edinburgh in a big way and imaginative chefs have taken the best that Scotland has to offer so that Aberdeen Angus beef, Loch Fyne oysters, fish and shellfish from the West Coast, fresh salmon and venison feature prominently. So does haggis (including a vegetarian variety made with lentils, kidney beans and oatmeal). Many café-bars serve coffee, Mediterranean-style food, wine and light meals all day.

CAFES

There is no shortage of cafés serving excellent coffee, smoothies and cakes. You'll see all the usual High Street names (Costa Coffee, Café Nero, Starbucks) in and around the main shopping areas as well as many independent cafés. Here are a few of them.

Canongate, the Royal Mile; map F4–H3

Chocoholics will home in on Plaisir du Chocolat, a deeply civilized *salon du thé* at No. 251 where they can work their way through ten types of hot chocolate and toy with delicious patisseries, or nibble on brandy-filled praline shells. Lunches include smoked salmon with crème fraiche.

In contrast, Clarinda's (named for Robbie Burns's secret love) serves breakfast all day and homemade cakes.

Chambers Street; map E5

Café Delos at the Royal Museum of Scotland serves not only coffee and tea but also light lunches with local produce. You can try haggis with sweet potato here.

Charlotte Square; map A3

No. 28 is the smart café belonging to the National Trust for Scotland. Good light lunches, tea and coffee (and porridge with cream). Confusingly, part of it becomes No. 27 in the evenings when it is transformed into a

restaurant serving classic Scottish food.

Dundas Street; map C1

Coffee, tea or lunch is a pleasure at Glass and Thompson, a comfortable and airy licensed espresso bar, selling good cakes and sandwiches too.

Edinburgh Castle; map B5

The Queen Anne Café serves excellent light meals and coffee in part of the Castle that was once the Royal Gunhouse. Try their lightly buttered Selkirk bannocks.

Elm Row, Leith Walk; map F1

You must visit Valvona and Crolla, beloved Scottish-Italian deli, established for

Always Sunday

The Terrace Café

90 years and now a legend. It's sheer pleasure to walk through the floor-to-ceiling stocked shop to the café behind. It's a good bet you'll have to buy olive oil, chocolate, olives, pâtés, biscuits or cheese on the way out.

George IV Bridge; map D5

The Elephant House is another café beloved by locals. It stays open late with a good selection of sandwiches, cakes, quiches, teas and coffees in a huge room where you can linger over a newspaper.

High Street, Royal Mile; map D4–E4

Always Sunday is the cheerful name of this award-winning beautifully light and airy deli-type licensed café serving fair-trade coffee, home-made cakes and a good choice of deli food all day. They do hot dishes too. Just a step or two away is the High Kirk of St Giles with its Lower Aisle café, popular with Edinburgh's legal eagles from the nearby High Court. Home-baked cakes and scones and straightforward jacket potatoes, good soups and casseroles or kedgeree hit the spot nicely.

Howard Street, Canonmills

The Olive Branch deli (linked to the bistro in Broughton Street) is the place for tea, coffee or a light lunch if you're in this part of the New Town.

Inverleith Row

Food with a view is what you get at The Terrace Café at the Royal Botanic Gardens, just 15 minutes away from the city centre.

Queen Street; map D2
You don't have to see the art at the National Portrait Gallery (although you'd be missing a treat) to enjoy tea and scones with black-currant jam at the Queen Street Café inside. There's always an expectant crowd here at 10.30 each morning waiting for the freshly baked scones to come out of the oven.

RESTAURANTS AND BISTROS
Chinese
Loon Fung
2 Warriston Place
Cantonese food as it should be – try baked crab in ginger sauce or the crispy monkfish. Open until late.
Tel: 0131 556 1781

Fishers in the City

Mussel Inn

Fish
Creelers
3 Hunter Square; map E4
Run by the owners of a West Coast fishing busi-ness, this fine fish restau-rant offers dishes such as hake with nori seaweed, seafood chowder and home-smoked fish.
Tel: 0131 220 4447

Fishers in the City
58 Thistle Street; map C2
From simple chowder or fishcakes to langoustine or oysters, the excellent fish here is fresh and beauti-fully served.
Tel: 0131 225 5109

Mussel Inn
61–65 Rose Street; map C3
Owned by Scottish shell-fish farmers, this popular restaurant serves mussels and chips – and other dishes – with panache.
Tel: 0131 225 5979

French
Café Marlayne
76 Thistle Street; map C2
Classic French country cooking (such as Toulouse sausages in mustard sauce) in this small city-centre bistro where the menu changes each day.
Tel: 0131 226 2230

Café St Honoré
34 North West Thistle Street Lane; map C2
Cosy restaurant where you can sample lamb shank with spinach and boudin noir; turbot in cider and aubergine; or red onion, tomato and goat's cheese crumble.
Tel: 0131 226 2211

La Garrigue
31 Jeffrey Street; map F4
A very upmarket restaurant, specializing in regional cooking from the Languedoc. The food is excellent, from traditional fish soup with rouille and croutons to braised lamb shank with regional sausage and herbs. Puddings include fresh figs baked with blackberries with a muscat wine custard.
Tel: 0131 557 3032

Italian
Gennaro
64 Grassmarket; map D5
Pizzas, pastas, salads, seafood, veal, steak and fish dishes at this cheerful restaurant in the heart of the Old Town.
Tel: 0131 226 3706

Mediterranean/fusion/modern Scottish cooking
Café Hub
Lawnmarket; map D4
Colourful and bustling, blue and yellow bistro café in the Edinburgh Festival Centre. Light meals, such as noodles, and snacks all day and most evenings.
Tel: 0131 473 2067

Café Hub

Maison Bleue

OLD AND NEW

Edinburgh's New Town, with its classic grid design and neo-classical architecture, came about when the city's overcrowding became a problem. In 1767 the 23-year-old James Craig won a competition to design several new, elegant streets for the city.

The Grain Store

Howies
29 Waterloo Place;
map E3

'Fine food without the faff' is the motto of all four Howies restaurants in Edinburgh (find the others in Victoria Street, map D5, Bruntsfield Road, and Glanville Place, Stockbridge). You'll find dishes like spinach, lemon and lentil soup; tian of crab, avocado and lime with a cardamom syrup; and parfait of duck liver and smoked bacon with braised sultana compote.
Tel: 0131 556 5766

Maison Bleue
36–38 Victoria Street;
map D5

Order as many medium-sized portions as you fancy to sample a wide range of food from haggis balls in beer batter to scallop brochettes and venison.
Tel: 0131 226 1900

Ricks
55a Frederick Street;
map B3

Ricks restaurant is flexible about serving food, so that at any time of day you can enjoy a light breakfast, slurp half a dozen oysters

or fill up with a three-course meal. It's popular with locals and visitors.
Tel: 0131 622 7800

The Grain Store
30 Victoria Street; map D5

Don't walk past the unassuming entrance of this restaurant, which serves top quality local produce, freshly cooked. You'll find salmon, beef, venison, game, fresh fish and seafood on the menu. Try the celeriac soup, mussel risotto with saffron and dill, or the pork rillette to start; then sample seared

salmon with a basil
veloute – or confit and
breast of guinea fowl with
spring cabbage and whole
grain mustard.
Tel: 0131 225 7635

The Olive Branch

The Olive Branch
**91 Broughton Street;
map E1**
Small and friendly café-bar
serving all-day food, hot
chocolate and coffee, and
a small à la carte evening
menu, which includes
dishes such as chicken
marinated in coriander
with a vegetable salsa,
vegetable hot-pot, and red
mullet. Loudish – but not
overwhelming – music and
excellent service.
Tel: 0131 557 4265

The Point
34 Bread Street
Restaurant belonging to a
classic modern hotel off
Lothian Road. Crisp, white
tablecloths, smart service
and fresh local food at a
reasonable price.
Tel: 0131 221 5555

The Tower
**Museum of Scotland,
Chambers Street; map E5**
Under the same owner-
ship as The Witchery,
this classy restaurant on
level 5 of the Museum of
Scotland has views right
across to the Castle, which
is floodlit at night. Food
includes top quality local
beef, venison, oysters
and scallops.
Tel: 0131 225 3003

The Warehouse Bar
and Grill
**99 Hanover Street;
map C2**
Smart surroundings and
good food, including
dishes such as Parma ham
and Emmental tart; pan-
fried chicken breast with
bean and Parmesan mash;
and loin of lamb with rosti.
Tel: 0131 225 8700

The Witchery by the
Castle
Castlehill; map D4

Eating in this gloriously
Gothic restaurant, or its
equally beautiful 'sister',
The Secret Garden, also in
Castlehill, may be expen-
sive, but worth it for the

The Secret Garden at The Witchery

almost over-the-top dining room, wood-panelled and furnished, it seems, with redundant bits of old churches, chubby gilded cherubs, tapestries and stone. Set lunches at The Secret Garden are delicious and good value at around £10 (although once you've had drinks and added on pudding and coffee the price soars). You might be offered leek and seafood bisque or Roquefort tart for starters, with beef daube followed by plum tarte tatin for dessert or crème brulée in various assorted flavours.
Tel: 0131 225 5613

Spanish
Iggs
15 Jeffrey Street; map F4
This elegant restaurant and its adjoining tapas bar, La Barioja, has accrued a formidable reputation for food such as fillets of sea bass with celeriac purée, braised fennel and cherry tomatoes, air-dried Spanish meats and roast butternut squash, red lentil and coconut milk soup.
Tel: 0131 557 8184

The Tapas Tree
1 Forth Street; map E4

Cheerful and friendly tapas bar with an amazing variety of pinchos (skewers) containing delicacies such as venison marinated in red wine, chargrilled chicken and roasted vegetables. There's paella, casserole of pork with sweet peppers and roasted spare ribs. Some evenings there's flamenco and live guitar too.
Tel: 0131 556 6766

Thai
Thai Me Up in Edinburgh
4 Picardy Place; map E1
Ignore the jokey name – those who have lived in Thailand say the food here is the real thing.
Tel: 0131 558 9234

Vegetarian
David Bann
56–58 St Mary's Street; map F4
Call in for imaginative snacks, lunch or dinner. You'll find grilled red pepper and basil polenta with goat's cheese and black olive tapenade; or wild mushroom with fresh ginger and teriyaki layered with sticky coconut rice and wrapped in seaweed, while puddings include white chocolate brulée.
Tel: 0131 556 5888

Henderson's
94 Hanover Street; map C3
Janet Henderson set up a vegetarian deli and subsequently a restaurant over

Henderson's

40 years ago, before such things were common. Now the Henderson's empire stretches to a bistro, a wine bar and a deli – all vegetarian – next door to each other and very popular too. Call in for fresh food made from organic, GM-free ingredients, following the Henderson philosophy 'eat better, live better'.
Tel: 0131 225 2131

The Bow Bar

PUBS

Edinburgh is full of good pubs. Here are a few to choose from.

Abbotsford, Rose Street; map D3

This atmospheric Victorian pub, all wood panelling and polished brass, once belonged to Jenners department store. Its island bar serves local guest beers while there's lunchtime bar food and a restaurant upstairs.

Barony Bar, Broughton Street; map E1

Nice old-fashioned feel to this traditional pub in what is now a trendy part of town. Good food but you might have to wait as it's very popular.

The Bow Bar, West Bow; map D5

You come to this beautiful-looking wood-panelled pub to drink rather than eat, although they do rolls and toasties to soak up the effects of excellent cask-strength malts and well-kept real ales.

Café Royal

Café Royal, West Register Street; map D2

Another Victorian bar just off St Andrew Square with a huge island bar counter and tiles portraying famous inventors, such as Watt, Caxton and Faraday. Excellent food, beer, wine and malt whisky.

Canon's Gait, Canongate; map F4

Despite the jokey name this is a smart Royal Mile pub with a good atmosphere, lunchtime food and real ale.

Guildford Arms, West Register Street; map D2

More Victorian cosiness off St Andrew Square with velvet curtains, decorated glass and dark wood. Good gallery-type restaurant that gives a view of the drinkers below.

Kay's Bar, Jamaica Street; map B2

Once a wine and whisky shop this is a small, well-kept pub with lots of atmosphere and a blazing fire if the weather's a bit drear. Tasty lunchtime food and cask beers.

Last Drop, Grassmarket; map C5

The rather grim pun on this traditional old pub's name is a reminder that it stands just feet from the site of Edinburgh's gallows, where crowds would gather to watch public executions. Now you go for a relaxing pint and something to eat.

Milne's Bar, Hanover Street; map C3

Some of the original character of the 'poets' pub' remains from the days

Milne's Bar

when poets Hugh McDiarmid, Sorley Maclean and Sydney Goodyear Smith used to meet in the Little Kremlin room here.

Standing Order, George Street; map C3

Grand conversion by Wetherspoons of this former bank into a trendy town pub with several rooms (one with a genuine Adam fireplace).

Guildford Arms

Kay's Bar

Last Drop

AN EVENING OUT

Everyone's heard of Edinburgh's widely acclaimed Traverse Theatre – but there are others too. The city seems never to sleep during the Festival in August, although the performing arts are well served during the rest of the year. There is a thriving club scene too, and a range of cinemas and comedy clubs.

Stage ...

You can call in at The Hub, the city's Festival Centre at Castlehill (map D4), for information all year round. Call 0131 473 2000.

The Bedlam Theatre, a converted church in Forrest Road (past Greyfriars Kirk), is the only one in the country fully run by students. But that's not to say it's not professional and interesting. Call 0131 225 9893 or visit www.eusa.ed.ac.uk/bedlam.

The Edinburgh Playhouse is next door to the Theatre Royal Bar, which is adorned with gilded heralds, in Greenside Place (map F1). This huge theatre shows popular West-End hits and musicals. Call 0131 557 2692 or visit www.cclive.co.uk.

The Festival Theatre in Nicolson Street has an enormous stage, a good size for its many operatic productions. Call 0131 529 6000 or visit its website www.eft.co.uk.

The Royal Lyceum in Grindlay Street (map A5) can be relied on for a good mainstream performance. Call 0131 248 4800 or visit www.lyceum.org.uk.

For more than 40 years the Traverse Theatre has been a showcase for new writing and experimental theatre. It's in Cambridge Street (map B5). Call 0131 228 1404 or visit www.traverse.co.uk.

You should find something to laugh about at The Stand Comedy Club in York Place (map D2) where each programme features around five acts. Call 0131 558 7272 or visit www.thestand.co.uk.

... and screen

If you're into art-house movies go to Cameo (tel: 0131 228 4141), a three-

Theatre Royal Bar

style, is in a smart building in Holyrood Road (map G4). Honeycomb (tel: 0131 220 4381) in Niddry Street (map E4) attracts a sophisticated crowd, while hordes of people go to Club Java (tel: 0131 467 3810) in a converted church in Commercial Street, Leith.

Live music
Jazz is on offer every night at Henry's Jazz Bar (tel: 0131 221 1288) in Morrison Street (off Lothian Road), while The Liquid Room (tel: 0131 225 2528) in Victoria Street (map D5) is a clubby venue with a mix of bands. Whistleblinkies (tel: 0131 557 5114) on South Bridge (map E4) has rock, pop and folk most nights. Wall-to-wall folk is on offer at Sandy Bell's (tel: 0131 225 2751) in Forrest Road.

screen cinema in Home Street, or Filmhouse (tel: 0131 228 2688), the main venue for the annual Film Festival in Lothian Road (map A5).

The Dominion (tel: 0131 447 4771) in Newbattle Terrace shows all the new

releases and there are Odeons in Clerk Street and Lothian Road (tel: 0870 505 0007).

Go clubbing
Edinburgh favourite, The Bongo Club (tel: 0131 558 7604), famous for its innovative underground

You can listen to classical music at St Cecilia's Hall (tel: 0131 650 2805) in Niddry Street (map E4), at The Queen's Hall (tel: 0131 667 2019) in Clerk Street and at the Usher Hall (tel: 0131 228 1155) at the Grindlay Street end of Lothian Road (map A5).

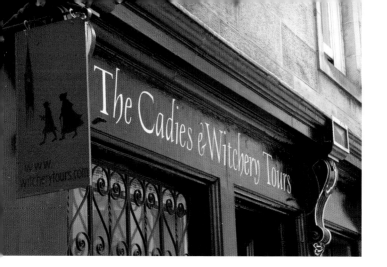

TOURS AND TRIPS

The best way to explore Edinburgh is on foot, although it is not a bad idea to get a feel for the city by taking one of the entertaining and informative open-top bus tours that depart regularly from Waverley Bridge (map D3). Different companies operate from here but the ticket prices are much the same (under £10) and you can get off the bus to see whatever takes your fancy, and hop on again any time in the next 24 hours. Buy your ticket from the booth by the bridge, or on the bus.

Be very afraid
You will be by the time you've taken part in almost any one of the many entertaining, but mostly scary, walking tours of the city. There are a lot, but one of the favourites is the Black Hart Story-tellers City of the Dead

haunted graveyard tour, which will have you whimpering in seconds. It leaves the Royal Mile (next to St Giles) nightly. Call 0131 225 9044 or visit www.blackhart.com.

Then there are the hugely entertaining but spooky Cadies and Witchery Tours (0131 225 6745; www.witcherytours.com). Cadies were the little lads who ran errands and guided visitors safely through the narrow closes and wynds of the Old Town. Times vary, but the meeting point is outside The Witchery restaurant in Castlehill (map D4).

Mercat Tours, which leave from the Mercat Cross in the High Street (call 0131 557 6464 or visit www.mercattours.com), will give away the secrets of the Royal Mile and its ghosts, while Auld Reekie Tours offer more scary walks (call 0131 557 4700 or visit the website www.auldreekietours.co.uk).

Literary and other rambles
The Edinburgh Literary Pub Tour combines tales of Edinburgh's mighty writers with a good old-fashioned pub crawl. Contact them on 0131 226 6665. If you're an Ian Rankin fan, you'll be interested in the Rebus Tours, based on Rankin's best-selling Inspector Rebus novels. Details of the two walks on offer are on www.rebustours.com.

If you don't like horror, go for the Leith Walks, run by guide Tim Bell. You can contact him on 0131 555 2500, or look at www.leithwalks.co.uk.

Much more serious, specialist and strenuous, but very informative, are the Geowalks – often day-long excursions – run by Angus Miller (tel: 0131 555 5488; website: www.geowalks.demon.co.uk). An expert explains the geology of the region.

Cycle the city
The twice-daily cycle tours of Edinburgh are very popular. They each last three hours, are leisurely, and cost around £15 (£5 for children) including hire of the bike and helmet. They start at the gates of Holyrood Palace at the bottom of the Royal Mile (map H3). Call 07966 447 206 to book, or find more information on www.edinburghcycletour.com.

Hike the Highlands
Walkabout Scotland, run by Paul Mason and Jon Haber, will pick you up from Edinburgh for a stimulating hike – about 8–10 kilometres (5–6 miles) – in some of Scotland's loveliest scenery. Call them on 0131 661 7168 for details or visit www.walkaboutscotland.com.

B O D Y S N A T C H E R S
Edinburgh's Grassmarket is an open, sunny spot, a good place to sit at a pavement café and watch the world go by. It wasn't always so – public executions were held here and the notorious murderers Burke and Hare lured their victims to their lair in the Grassmarket before strangling them and selling the bodies to medics for dissection.

WHAT'S ON

Well – there's the Edinburgh Festival and the Fringe Festival of course, but it doesn't stop there. Edinburgh doesn't close down at any time of the year and there are celebrations and events happening throughout.

As well as the websites and contact the numbers given here, the Tourist Information Centre (tel: 0845 2255 121; www.edinburgh.org) and www.theoracle.co.uk and www.eventful-edinburgh.com give lots of information.

31 Dec–1 Jan
Edinburgh Hogmanay
This is claimed to be the world's favourite place to celebrate the New Year – nowhere else in the world do so many people sing 'Auld Lang Syne' on the stroke of midnight.
Website: www.edingburghshogmanay.org

April
Ceilidh Culture
A month-long festival of world music including concerts and workshops.
Tel: 0131 478 8446
Website: www.ceilidhculture.co.uk

International Science Festival
Twelve days of experiments, talks, and shows – science for everyone.
Tel: 0131 558 7666
Website: www.sciencefestival.co.uk

Easter Festival
Fabulous Easter parade throughout the city and other events.
Website: www.edinburghparade.co.uk

Puppet Animation Festival
Performances and workshops from worldwide puppet companies.
Tel: 0131 556 9579

May
Children's Theatre Festival
Britain's biggest performing arts event for children, with international participants.
Tel: 0131 225 8050
Website: www.imaginate.org.uk

June
Leith Festival
Visits to historic buildings, tours, recitals, walks and a gala to celebrate Leith.
Website: www.leithfestival.com

The Great Scottish Walk
Around 5,000 people take part in this charity walk of 10 or 20 kilometres (6 or 12 miles) around the city.
Tel: 08702 402 018
Website: www.greatscottishwalk.com

Royal Highland Show
The best of Scotland's country industry takes the

opportunity to show itself off here.
Tel: 0131 335 6236
Website: www.royalhighlandhshow.org

July

The Edinburgh International Jazz and Blues Festival

Emphasis on traditional jazz at this nine-day event.
Website: www.jazzmusic.co.uk

August

The Edinburgh Military Tattoo

Massed bands in front of Edinburgh Castle.
Tel: 08707 555 1188
Website: www.edintattoo.co.uk

The Edinburgh Festival Fringe

The world's largest arts

Festival Fringe office

event with thousands of performances.
Tel: 0131 226 0000
Website: www.edfringe.com

The Edinburgh International Film Festival

Best new films on show, as well as retrospectives, documentaries and talks.
Tel: 0131 229 2550
Websites: www.edfilmfest.org.uk

The Edinburgh International Book Festival

Two weeks of literary celebration with top authors from around the world.
Tel: 0131 624 5050
Website: www.edbookfest.co.uk

The Edinburgh International Festival

Opera, ballet, music and theatre from the world's leading companies.
Tel: 0131 473 2001
Website: www.eif.co.uk

International Television Festival

Annual festival for the broadcasting industry.
Tel: 020 7430 1333
Website: www.getif.corpex.com

September

Mela

Multi-cultural celebration that mixes music, art and dance from India, Pakistan, Africa, Bangladesh, China and Scotland.
Tel: 0131 557 1400
Website: www.edinburgh-mela.co.uk

October

Storytelling Festival

Not only for children, this festival celebrates music, legend, myth and stories from Scottish culture.
Tel: 0131 557 5724
Website: www.scottishstorytellingcentre.co.uk

November

Fiddle Festival

Three days of recitals, workshops and master classes to get the feet tapping.
Tel: 0131 228 1155
Website: www.scotsfiddlefestival.com

December

Edinburgh's Capital Christmas

Lots of Christmas events, including markets and readings of Dickens.
Website: www.edinburghcapitalchristmas.org

EDINBURGH FOR KIDS

No matter what your youngsters are into, you'll find something to keep them happily occupied in Edinburgh. There's plenty of open space (see pages 56–57) for them to let off steam, too.

Animal magic

Edinburgh Zoo, at Murrayfield just 5 kilometres (3 miles) to the west of the city on the A8 and easily accessible by bus from Princes Street, has more than 1,000 animals ranging from tiny, blue poison-arrow frogs to rhinos. There are lessons to be learned here about endangered species and lots of fun to be had in the Evolution Maze and the Magic Forest. You may also be lucky enough to see the penguin parade.
Open: daily; Apr–Sep: 9.00–18.00; Oct and Mar: 9.00–17.00; Nov–Feb: 9.00–16.30
Entry: under £10
Tel: 0131 334 9171
Website: www. edinburghzoo.org.uk

There's a hands-on approach to animals at the Gorgie City Farm, 3 kilometres (2 miles) west of the city centre in Gorgie Road, near the Hearts football ground. There's a picnic and play area, lots of ducks, sheep, hens and rabbits and a good café. Take a bus from Princes Street or drive along the A71 and follow the signs.
Open: daily; summer 9.30–16.30, winter 9.30–16.00
Entry: free
Tel: 0131 538 7263
Website: www. activitypoint.co.uk

Did you know that a butterfly that enjoys a yummy diet of mud, dung and rotting fruit will live longer than a nectar-sipper? This and other fascinating facts about butterflies and creepy-crawlies are on offer at Edinburgh Butterfly and Insect World, to the south of the city off the A720 city bypass at the Gilmerton exit. It is situated within Dobbie's Garden World and well sign-posted.

Edinburgh Zoo

The Museum of Scotland

Open: daily; Apr–Oct:
9.30–17.30; Nov–Mar:
10.00–17.00
Entry: around £5
Tel: 0131 663 4932
Website: www.
edinburgh-butterfly-
world.co.uk

Learning zone
The Museum of Scotland
(see pages 43–44) was
designed with children
very much in mind – from
the layout itself (spiral
staircases, balconies and a
see-through lift) to the
interactive displays. Young
people can follow special
routes, tracking certain
objects and solving
puzzles. Next door at the
linked Royal Museum (see
page 50) is the amazing
Millennium Clock and a
child-friendly café.

The great outdoors
Kids of all ages enjoy
exploring the Royal
Botanic Garden (see page
48) where there are
jungles in glasshouses,
acres of space and a
terrace café that
welcomes youngsters.

NOT SO TASTEFUL
Children will love
the gruesome
Roman sculpture of
a lioness devouring a
poor hapless human.
The large carved
piece, discovered
by ferryman Rob
Graham in
the River Almond at
Cramond in January
1997, is now on
display in the
Museum of Scotland
in Chambers Street.

Hopetoun House

OUT OF TOWN

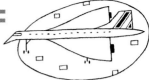

It might be hard to tear yourself away from the city but there are many splendid places to visit nearby. Here are some of them.

Cramond

3 miles north-west of the city centre off the A902

Cramond is the upmarket village where writer Muriel Spark situated the turreted house of Miss Jean Brodie's lover, Gordon Lowther, in her sparkling novel. It is still a lovely village and a good starting point for pleasant walks. Be sure to visit the Cramond Gallery Bistro down by the River Almond, where you can have a Miss Jean Brodie cream tea, Scots lemon tart (Lady Tweedsmore recipe, 1820) or Ecclefechan tart (Meg Dodds' recipe, 1826) and learn all about the Roman occupation of Cramond from Crammond Gallery owner Alan Bogue.

Hopetoun House

Near South Queensferry, 12 miles north-west of

Cramond

Edinburgh off the A90 and A904

This Georgian house is more than 400 years old. It was built by Holyroodhouse architect William Bruce with additions by William Adam, and claims to be Scotland's finest stately home. Regular visitors go not only for the fine paintings, tapestries and furniture, but also for a visit to the splendid tearooms where you can order a traditional Scottish tea or an ultra-special champagne tea.
Tel: 0131 331 2451
Website: www. hopetounhouse.com

Edinburgh Zoo

Corstorphine Road, 2¹/₂ miles west of the city centre off the A8, Glasgow Road

The zoo (see also page 86) is home to a number of endangered and rare species and offers a good family day out, with attractions such as the Magic Forest (small primates) and the watery Evolution Maze. You may see the penguin parade – a 'crocodile' of birds, led by their keeper, taking a waddling walk through the grounds.
Tel: 0131 334 9171
Website: www. edinburghzoo.org.uk

Little Sparta

Near the village of Dunsyre, 25 miles south-west of Edinburgh off the A702 (turn off at Dolphinton)

Go singly and silently into this most thoughtful and moving of gardens, said by some to be the most original in the country. Poet and artist Ian Hamilton Finlay has created this garden in the Pentland Hills over the last 40 years. It will evoke strong feelings and will stay with you long after you've walked down the long stony path back to your car. It's open on Friday and Sunday afternoons from June to September only.
Tel: 01899 810252

Craigmillar Castle

Craigmillar, 3 miles to the east of the city centre, off the A7

Mary Queen of Scots is said to have stayed at Craigmillar so often that the surrounding area became known as Little France. There's no doubt that this castle was the base for the plotters involved in the murder of Lord Darnley, the queen's husband.
Tel: 0131 661 4445
Website: www.caledoniancastles.co.uk

Portobello

3 miles east of the city centre on the A1

This little seaside town with its sandy beach was the birthplace of singer Sir Harry (Roamin' in the Gloamin') Lauder. There's a plaque to that effect on his old family house in Bridge Street. The very un-Scottish name commemorates a naval victory over Puerto Bello in Panama.

Museum of Flight

East Fortune Airfield, East Lothian, 20 miles east of Edinburgh sign-posted from the A1 near Haddington

One of the biggest draws here is the recently arrived Concorde which has undergone restoration and is now open to visitors. You can get close to more than 50 other aircraft – military, recreational and civilian – and find out about the enormous changes that flight has brought to our lives.
Tel: 01620 880 308
Website: www.nms.ac.uk

Little Sparta

WHERE TO STAY

The Witchery
Apartments

Whatever the time of year people flock to Edinburgh, so it's hardly surprising to find a huge range of accommodation. The Tourist Information Centre (see page 94) has a complete list of hotels, guest houses, bed and breakfasts, pubs, self-catering accommodation and caravan and camp sites. The list below will give you some idea of the range on offer. Check facilities and prices before booking.

Prices

The £ symbols are an approximate guide for comparing the prices charged for bed and breakfast, which range from £50 to more than £150 per twin or double room per night.

The Balmoral
1 Princes Street; map E3

This is the grandest hotel in town with 168 rooms and 20 suites, a swimming pool, gym, two good restaurants and even a kilted doorman.
Tel: 0131 556 2414
Website: www.rfhotels.com
££££

Doorman at
The Balmoral

The Scotsman
20 North Bridge; map E3

The marble staircase and walnut panelling of the wonderful old newspaper offices of *The Scotsman* have been retained, but you'll find 56 bedrooms (fancy sleeping in the editor's room or the publisher's suite?) and 12 suites furnished in contemporary style and materials. There are also leisure facilities and two very good restaurants.
Tel: 0131 556 5565
Website: www.thescotsmanhotel.co.uk
££££

The Witchery Apartments
Castlehill; map D4

Theatrical, opulent, luxurious, probably over-the-top but certainly unforgettable, these seven suites full of antique furniture and top of the range music systems also feature roll-top baths – for two.
Tel: 0131 225 5613
Website: www.thewitchery.com
££££

Rick's Restaurant with Rooms
55a Frederick Street; map B3

Ten sophisticated and comfortable rooms attached to this popular restaurant in the heart of the New Town.
Tel: 0131 622 7800
Website: www.ricksedinburgh.co.uk
£££

26 Gayfield Square

This comfortable and welcoming family home in an elegant Georgian Square has just two rooms, each with its own bath. Less than five minutes' walk from Princes Street, it's perfect for a short break and you'll be offered proper porridge with breakfast. Good restaurants nearby.
Tel: 0131 556 5260
££

11 Warriston Crescent

26 Gayfield Square

decorated rooms and delicious breakfasts – always served with fresh fruit and home-made jams and compotes.
Tel: 0131 556 0093
££

Gladstone's Land
Lawnmarket; map D4
You've probably put this fine house on the Royal Mile on your list of places to visit and you can actually stay here too – if you book well in advance. The National Trust for Scotland rent out a two-roomed self-catering apartment, which you can book for a week in summer and a minimum of three nights in winter. It sleeps two.
Tel: 0131 243 9331
Website: www.nts.org.uk
££

11 Warriston Crescent
The owner of this lovely old Georgian house just across the way from the Botanic Gardens is a garden designer – you can tell that by her own peaceful and pretty garden. Just two beautifully

Ashlyn Guest House
42 Inverleith Row
Comfortable, clean and friendly guest house with just eight bedrooms near the Botanic Gardens and a mile from Princes Street. From here, it's a pleasant walk or an easy bus ride into the centre of town. Good breakfasts.
Tel: 0131 552 2954
Website: www. ashlyn-edinburgh.com
£££

USEFUL INFORMATION

TOURIST INFORMATION

Tourist Information Centre (TIC)
3 Princes Street,
Edinburgh EH2 2QP;
map E3
Services include booking accommodation, travel, event and attraction information, maps and guides.
Open: Jul–Aug: Mon–Sat 9.00–20.00, Sun 10.00–20.00; May–Jun and Sep: Mon–Sat 9.00–19.00, Sun 10.00–19.00; Apr and Oct: Mon–Sat 9.00–18.00, Sun 10.00–18.00; Nov–Mar: Mon–Sat 9.00–17.00, Sun 10.00–16.00
Tel: 0845 2255 121
Website: www. edinburgh.org

WHAT'S ON

Check with the TIC or buy a copy of the fortnightly listings magazine *The List*, available at newsagents.

GUIDED WALKING TOURS

Auld Reekie Tours:
Tel: 0131 557 4700

Website: www. auldreekietours.co.uk
Cadies and Witchery Tours:
Tel: 0131 225 6745
Website: www. witcherytours.com
City of the Dead Tours:
Tel: 0131 225 9044
Website: www. blackhart.com
Edinburgh Literary Pub Tour:
Tel: 0131 226 6665
Website: www. edinburghliterarypubtour. co.uk
Leith Walks:
Tel: 0131 555 2500
Website: www. leithwalks.co.uk
Mercat Tours:
Tel: 0131 557 6464
Website: www. mercattours.com
Rebus Tours:
Website: www. rebustours.com
Geowalks:
Website: www. geowalks.demon.co.uk

TRAVEL

By air

Edinburgh International Airport is 8 miles west of the city centre at Turnhouse. Regular Airlink shuttles take you to Waverley Bridge in Princes Street for around £3.50. A taxi to the city costs around £15.
Airport: 0131 333 1000

By rail

Waverley Station is right in the centre of the city; map D3
National rail enquiries: 08457 484950

By car

Parking in Edinburgh is hard to find and very expensive. Restrictions are rigorously enforced by parking inspectors who are on duty 24 hours a day. If you can avoid bringing your car into the city you'll find that the bus and taxi system is relatively cheap and easy to use. Park at a railway station on the outskirts and travel into the city by train.

By coach and bus

Edinburgh's bus station is on the north-east corner

of St Andrew Square (map D2) with pedestrian entrances in Elder Street and North St Andrew Street.

Lothian Buses offer a day pass for around £2, which gives unlimited travel on their services for a day, and a weekly pass for around £10 (you'll need photographic proof of identity for the weekly pass). Passes and time-tables from the Lothian ticket centre on Waverley Bridge (map D3) or the Lothian travel shop at 27 Hanover Street (map C3). Tel: 0131 555 6363 First Edinburgh also offer day and weekly passes. Tel: 0131 663 9233.

Shopmobility
St Andrew Square; map D2
Lothian Shopmobility hires out electric buggies from a mobile unit to those with limited mobility. Telephone first to check location and arrange your buggy.
Tel: 0131 225 9559

Taxis
Edinburgh operates a black cab system and there are plenty of clearly marked ranks, or you can simply hail a cab in the street.

BANKS
Bank of Scotland, The Mound, map C4
Bank of Scotland, 38 St Andrew Square, map D2
Barclays, 1 St Andrew Square, map D2
HSBC, 76 Hanover Street, map C2
Lloyds TSB, 120 George Street, map B3
NatWest, 80 George Street, map C3
Royal Bank of Scotland, 42 St Andrew Square, map D2

POST OFFICE
The main Post Office is at 8–10 St James Centre, map E2

SPORT
Meadowbank Sports Centre, 139 London Road, has sports halls and athletic tracks;
Tel: 0131 661 5351
Rugby is played at Murrayfield Stadium, 2 miles to the west of the city centre;
Tel: 0131 346 5000
Swimming pools include the Royal Commonwealth, 21 Dalkeith Road;
Tel: 0131 667 7211

Glenogle Swim Centre, 3 Glenogle Road;
Tel: 0131 343 6376
Portobello Swim Centre, 57 Promenade, Portobello;
Tel: 0131 669 6888

EMERGENCIES
Fire, ambulance or police
Tel: 999

Police
Lothian and Borders Police HQ, Fettes Avenue
Tel: 0131 311 3131

Hospital
The Royal Infirmary at Little France, Old Dalkeith Road has a 24-hour casualty department
Tel: 0131 536 1000

Late-night pharmacy
Boots, 48 Shandwick Place stays open until 21.00 during the week
Tel: 0131 225 6757

24-hour breakdown service
24-7 Rescue and Recovery, 25 Laurie Street
Tel: 0131 555 5357

24-hour petrol station
Tesco, 30 Meadow Place Road
Tel: 0131 470 0700

INDEX

CITY-BREAK GUIDES

These full-colour guides come with stunning new photography capturing the essence of some of Britain's loveliest cities and towns. Each is divided into easy-reference sections where you will find something for everyone – from walk maps to fabulous shopping, from sightseeing highlights to keeping the kids entertained, from recommended restaurants to tours and trips ... and much, much more.

BATH

Stylish and sophisticated – just two adjectives that sum up the delightful Roman city of Bath, which saw a resurgence of popularity in Georgian times and in the 21st century is once again a vibrant and exciting place to be.

BRIGHTON

Famous for its piers, the magnificent Royal Pavilion, its huge choice of shops and restaurants and nightclubs, candyfloss and fairground rides, its shingly beach and deckchairs, its art, its culture – Brighton's got the lot.

CAMBRIDGE

Historic architecture mingles with hi-tech revolution in the university city of Cambridge, where stunning skylines over surrounding fenland meet the style and sophistication of modern city living.

CHESTER

Savour the historic delights of the Roman walls and charming black-and-white architecture, blending seamlessly with the contemporary shopping experience that make Chester such an exhilarating city.

OXFORD

City and university life intertwine in Oxford, with its museums, bookstores and all manner of sophisticated entertainment to entice visitors to its hidden alleyways, splendid quadrangles and skyline of dreaming spires.

STRATFORD

Universally appealing, the picturesque streets of Stratford draw visitors back time and again to explore Shakespeare's birthplace, but also to relish the theatres and stylish riverside town that exists today.

YORK

A warm northern welcome and modern-day world-class shops and restaurants await you in York, along with its ancient city walls, Viking connections and magnificent medieval Minster rising above the rooftops.

Jarrold Publishing, Healey House, Dene Road, Andover, Hampshire, SP10 2AA, UK
Sales: 01264 409206 Enquiries: 01264 409200 Fax: 01264 334110
e-mail: customer.services@jarrold-publishing.co.uk website: www.britguides.com

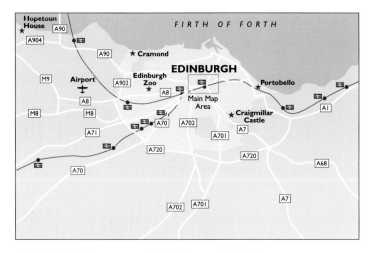

MAIN ROUTES IN AND OUT OF EDINBURGH

Places to visit out of town include:

Cramond
3 miles from the city
centre off the A902

Hopetoun House
12 miles from the city
centre off the A904

Edinburgh Zoo
2¹/₂ miles from the city
centre off the A8

Craigmillar Castle
3 miles from the city
centre off the A7

Portobello
3 miles from the city
centre on the A1

See pages 89–90 for
further details